TO LIVE MORE ABUNDANTLY

TO LIVE MORE

BLACK COLLEGIATE WOMEN, HOWARD UNIVERSITY

THE UNIVERSITY OF GEORGIA PRESS | ATHENS

ABUNDANTLY

ND THE AUDACITY OF DEAN LUCY DIGGS SLOWE

TAMARA BEAUBOEUF-LAFONTANT

TITLE PAGE IMAGE:
Dean Slowe with members of Howard University's Women's League, ca. 1930.
Courtesy of Scurlock Studio Records, Archives Center,
National Museum of American History,
Smithsonian Institution.

Designed by Kaelin Chappell Broaddus
Set in 11/13.5 Corundum Text Book by Kaelin Chaappell Broaddus

Most University of Georgia Press titles are
available from popular e-book vendors.

Printed digitally

Library of Congress Cataloging-in-Publication Data

Names: Beauboeuf-Lafontant, Tamara, author.
Title: To live more abundantly : Black collegiate women, Howard University,
and the audacity of Dean Lucy Diggs Slowe / Tamara Beauboeuf-Lafontant.
Description: Athens : The University of Georgia Press, [2022]
| Includes bibliographical references and index.
Identifiers: LCCN 2021031556 | ISBN 9780820361642 (Hardback) | ISBN
9780820361659 (Paperback) | ISBN 9780820361666 (eBook)
Subjects: LCSH: Slowe, Lucy Diggs, 1885–1937. | Educators—United States—Biography. |
African American women educators—Biography. | Women deans
(Education)—United States—Biography. | Howard University—History—
20th century. | Feminism and higher education—United States.
Classification: LCC LA2317.S6185 B43 2022 | DDC 378.009 [B]—dc23
LC record available at https://lccn.loc.gov/2021031556

FOR MY SISTER,
RÉGINE,
WHOSE JOY INSPIRES ME

CONTENTS

This project about the educational innovations of Lucy Diggs Slowe, dean of women at Howard University (1922–37), was sparked by a course I have taught for twenty years. First offered at DePauw University and more recently at Grinnell College, *Educating Women* takes a historical and topical approach to the contributions of diverse girls and women to primary, secondary, and higher education. My early enthusiasm for the course grew when I realized that I was on a campus with its own notable contributions to the history of coeducation: In the wake of the Civil War, DePauw became one of the first adopters of this contested social experiment. Moreover, in January 1870, four of its new women students—Bettie Locke, Bettie Tipton, Alice Allen, and Hannah Fitch—founded Kappa Alpha Theta, the first sorority for college women in the United States.

Despite DePauw's impressive historical place in the ongoing work of inclusion in higher education, more than a half-century—fifty-five years—passed between the admission of five white women in 1867 and the matriculation of two Black women, Valeria Murphy and Mattie Julian, in 1922.[1] This racial lag is all too familiar in the cause of education. In its self-knowledge and ongoing operations, higher education has been not only men centered but "persistently white."[2]

In my attempts to find more information about DePauw's first Black women students, the campus archivist, Wes Wilson, introduced me to the profession of dean of women. He suggested that I explore the materials of Katharine Sprague Alvord, who served as DePauw's dean of women from

1915 to 1936. Although deans of women were the early twentieth-century administrators who founded the contemporary field of student affairs, I had never heard of them. Moreover, despite Alvord's professional charge to attend to the personal growth of women students and the overlapping of her tenure with the undergraduate careers of Murphy and Julian, I found little about those women of color in the dean's papers. The absence of attention to these two pioneers alerted me to another significant fact: the whiteness of the deaning profession in its advocacy of the holistic—that is, the curricular and cocurricular—development of women students.

It was through my exploration of the history of deaning that I encountered Lucy Diggs Slowe, Alvord's contemporary and counterpart at Howard University as well as the first professionally trained African American dean of women in the United States. Slowe's was a name that I had come across on the periphery of other research projects. Within a few weeks, however, it became clear to me that she was an academic foremother whose story was both compelling and prescient.

There is much that draws me to Slowe. She was committed to the specific developmental moment of late adolescence and advocated for an expanded view of collegiate education. She, along with other deans, promoted self-governance, student-led interest groups, leisure activities, athletics, and vocational exploration as complements to the work undertaken in the classroom. I now better understand, and more deeply appreciate, the partnership that faculty should have with student affairs professionals to support our students' maturation into socially conscious citizens. I also have learned much from Dean Slowe about the importance of strong convictions, the need for sincere intergenerational and interracial relationships among women, and the possibilities that shared purpose unleashes. In Slowe I see a multifaceted educator whose guiding principle in her teaching and administrative labors was that Black women matter. As a result, she believed that they are worthy of our best efforts, which in higher education should include care, attention to the individual, expansive opportunities, and affirming community. That is, Slowe understood belonging as an institutional responsibility and a prerequisite for students' learning and growth. A century later her career offers a powerful vision of Black women thriving in, as well as transforming, higher education.

ACKNOWLEDGMENTS

To have an idea for a book is much different from actually completing it, and my community of support for this project has been extensive. I am indebted to many for their meaningful contributions to the book's realization:

* ✿ Dawn Durante, senior acquisitions editor at the University of Illinois Press. This project grew and matured under your care of honest feedback and patient encouragement. Thank you for continually seeing the possibilities just beyond my current focus.
* ✿ Marta Robertson, Elizabeth Stanley, Ilona Yim, Velma Garcia, Ginetta Candelario, Yvette Alex-Assensoh, Janie V. Ward, and Karla Erickson. As my writing family of choice, each of you has sustained this project by providing me with the accountability and reassurance I needed.
* ✿ The researchers at the Wellesley Centers for Women, especially Layli Maparyan, Sumru Erkut, Michelle Porsche, Jennifer Grossman, Linda Charmaraman, Amy Hoffman, and Peggy McIntosh. During my 2013–14 sabbatical, you provided me with a room of my own as well as wonderful intellectual company. You saw this book well before I could. It is now able to grace your shelves.
* ✿ Wes Wilson, DePauw University's coordinator of archives and special collections. In many ways this project began when you introduced me to the profession of dean of women. Thank you for guiding my first archival forays into this fascinating chapter in the history of higher education.

✣ The archival staff of Howard University's Moorland-Spingarn Research Center, especially Joellen ElBashir, curator; Alhaji Conteh, manuscript librarian; Sonja N. Woods, archivist; Richard Jenkins, library technician; and then–doctoral candidate Trevon Pegram. Your meticulous care of Dean Slowe's papers and generosity in making them available to me greatly eased my explorations of her historic career.

✣ Sarah Ryan, director of DePauw University's Women's Center and a passionate advocate for minoritized students. You move with the audacity of our dean of women foremothers, whose efforts made our careers possible. Thank you for your keen interest in Dean Slowe and her legacy.

✣ DePauw University's Faculty Development Program. A 2014–17 Faculty Fellowship granted me the time and resources essential for conducting the background research on the early history of coeducation, the emergence of deaning as a profession, and the career of Lucy Diggs Slowe. As always, I appreciate the program's investment in my growth.

✣ Mick Gusinde-Duffy, executive editor for scholarly and digital publishing at the University of Georgia Press. As with my first book, you intuitively grasped this project and brought it to completion. I appreciate your trust in me and belief in Dean Slowe.

✣ My family—Pascal, Dominique, and Milo. You accommodated my multiple workstations and graciously overlooked boxes of archival copies in our home. I am thankful to each of you for offering timely encouragement and the space I needed to grow new ideas.

This text expands on arguments that first appeared in the following:

Beauboeuf-Lafontant, Tamara. "The New Howard Woman: Lucy Diggs Slowe and the Education of a Modern Black Femininity." *Meridians* 17.1 (2018): 25–48.

TO LIVE MORE ABUNDANTLY

A "TWENTIETH CENTURY WONDER"

> In those days Howard University was essentially a man's university which included women in its student body and faculty. Dean Slowe's philosophy included the idea that women were beings in their own right and as independent beings had a purpose and function. The Women's Dinner was an early demonstration of this idea.
>
> **—Hilda Davis, class of 1925, Howard University**

On November 1, 1922, a public letter addressed to "the Men of the University" circulated among students, faculty, and administrators at Howard University. Its purpose was to inform them of an unprecedented women-only event taking place in two days' time. It opened with these words: "The women of the University are having a dinner Friday night, November 3, in the new dining hall. One of the requirements for admittance to this dinner is that you be a member of the female sex. This naturally bars all men in the University, with the possible exclusion of the waiters, from the floor of the dining hall."

The authors of this letter—the newly assembled Women's Committee on the First Annual Women's Dinner—reveled in their event's gender-exclusive design. Adopting a tone that was both confident and teasing, they feigned regret that the men would miss a striking example of "how much fun we women can have when you men are not present." Following this pronouncement, the planning committee offered a consolation: After 8:00 p.m. on Friday night, the men could "stand in the balcony of the dining hall to look down on us. From this, your point of vantage, you can force us women to do the usual thing: look up to you." However, even

Howard University Women's Dinner, 1940.
Courtesy of Scurlock Studio Records, Archives Center,
National Museum of American History, Smithsonian Institution.

this concession was wrapped in the women's glee. The onlooking men, the women predicted, would witness "'a twentieth century wonder,' Howard women enjoying themselves without the company of the men."[1]

The inaugural Women's Dinner did take place, with 250 students, alumnae, faculty, and guests in attendance. Not only did they take up space, they were audible in occupying it. As a student reported in the alumni magazine, the *Howard University Record*: "There were songs, 'screams,' as Dean Slowe is wont to call feminine attempts at yelling, and wonderfully inspiring speeches directed by the remarkably gifted toastmistress, Miss Bertha McNeil[l], and the students who would sing 'Stand Up' to whomsoever they wished to speak. From Dean Slowe's speech that set forth her high conception of the women's 'job' in the University throughout the entire list there was help and inspiration."[2]

At an event of their own making, on a patriarchal campus in the racially segregated city of Washington, D.C., these Black women defied many ex-

pectations of what was publicly possible for them. Bringing together Howard women across cohorts and formal standing, the inaugural Women's
Dinner foregrounded their sense of self and forms of engagement—sing-
ing, chants, and speeches—that were embodied, voiceful, proud, and community building. These women validated their claim that they were bringing into existence a "twentieth century wonder," and the Women's Dinner
soon became a cherished tradition among them. Held the first Friday in
November throughout Slowe's fifteen-year tenure, it remained an antici-
pated and vibrant site of pleasure and affirmation that Howard students
and alumnae sustained for another thirty years after Slowe's death in 1937.[3]

So who was the woman who envisioned and organized the Women's Dinner? In the opening decades of the twentieth century, Lucy Diggs Slowe
(1883–1937) was the first African American with professional training to
serve as dean of women. A 1908 Howard University alumna, she held a
master's degree from Columbia University and pursued postgraduate
coursework in the profession of deaning, the field that gave rise to what
we now know as student affairs. A pioneer in her profession, Slowe promoted equality, opportunity, and intrinsic worth across the lines of gender, color, and age. She believed that Black college women at Howard and
throughout higher education should experience rigorous and broad academic preparation, as well as extracurricular leadership opportunities, encouragement to pursue vocations of their choosing, and intra- and interracial racial gender solidarity. Slowe's educational vision rejected outdated
standards of respectability for women and racialized limits to campus belonging. She insisted that Black college women needed, and deserved to
develop, their individual talents and decide—for themselves—what contributions to make to society.

   The spirit of the Women's Dinner dramatically reflects Dean Slowe's
educational philosophy of "living more abundantly." This phrase comes
from a line in her eulogy by Dr. Dwight O. W. Holmes, a Black educator-
administrator. Holmes had known the fifty-four-year-old Slowe for a majority of her life, having served as her high school teacher, her administrative colleague at Howard University, and at times her confidant.[4] "Living
more abundantly" poetically distilled the motivation for Slowe's work—

her fervent belief in Black women's right to grow into their abilities and potential. As Holmes correctly assessed, Slowe's ideals of self-respect, self-determination, and community—key pillars of living more abundantly—were "not decorations but objectives to be actually achieved."[5] Through purposefully designed spaces and opportunities, Slowe and the college women for whom she advocated cultivated their own sense of self and departed from other people's reductive expectations of them.

Slowe understood the injustices of U.S. society. As she expressed in a set of personal essays, white domination and patriarchal attitudes created blocked opportunities and failures of recognition that left her feeling like a "woman without a country."[6] In orienting her work toward an aspirational society, Slowe contested disparagements of Black college women's abilities and asserted their "rightful place in American life" as full citizens with economic and political liberties.[7] As a result, Slowe pressed for their access not only to the academic curriculum but also to growth, joy, connection, and belonging in this developmental period of their lives. Holding to the view that Black college women were indisputably valuable modern persons, Slowe created visible, celebratory, and responsive environments for them. In this work she refuted racist and patriarchal devaluations of Black women's individual worth and social possibility. She also insisted on the socially regenerative possibilities of higher education. Core to her effort was her "faith in young people and . . . a belief in the mutability of human nature."[8] In short, Slowe's "living more abundantly" was both a validating educational philosophy for Black college women and a staunch rejection of pressures to accommodate them to lesser forms of inclusion and personhood.

Beyond Respectability
The New Negro Woman

The Women's Dinner was an audacious event to hold at a historically Black college or university (HBCU) in the 1920s. For African American college women a century ago, engaging in shows of respectability would have been more socially normative. From the wake of the Civil War into the early decades of the twentieth century, respectability was a dominant strategy for accessing the opportunities and protections of citizenship.[9] Upheld as a solution to U.S. racial problems, respectability predicated social inclusion on embodying white-defined norms of civil society. Despite its charge to all African Americans to demonstrate their social fitness, the discourse of racial respectability singled Black women out for heightened responsibilities. It maintained that Black women's work—a kind of "res(ex)pectability labor"—was to individually disprove a series of pejorative, white-constructed images of their womanhood that assailed their virtue, intelligence, and social worth.[10] Furthermore, as racial respectability also supported the establishment of Black men within masculine codes of power, it placed Black women under evaluative scrutiny within both their communities and society at large.

Respectability charged educated Black women in particular with demonstrating bourgeois characteristics of thrift, cleanliness, patriarchal homes, and a restrained heterosexuality. Living as exemplars, such women were expected to instill these qualities in the working classes, whose lives problematically appeared to validate white notions of Black racial deficit.[11] Because educated Black women were to confine their uplift labors to role modeling as opposed to active, visible leadership, a majority of them operated within the constraints of "the black woman's sphere—motherhood, teaching, and the helping professions."[12]

Although respectability did not necessarily define Black women in their own eyes, using it as a tool for navigating oppressive cultural and social dynamics did often require them to dissemble, or mask their true feelings with socially palatable appearances.[13] Such expectations that Black women would comport themselves to placate more socially advantaged others—whether whites or Black men—came at a cost to their own self-expression and self-knowledge. Given respectability's emphasis on Black women's displays of propriety, domesticity, community care, and support for men's leadership, some Black feminists view respectability as an "iron cage" and a "paradox" that secured, rather than undermined, the social dominance accorded men and whites.[14] For these reasons racial respectability was a discourse of Black womanhood that Slowe challenged throughout her career. She considered it an impediment to, and the antithesis of, "living more abundantly."

In much of its activity and tone, the Women's Dinner moved well beyond the codes of respectability, but it was very much in line with the tenets of New Negro Womanhood. This alternative movement for self-definition and full citizenship overlapped with respectability but focused on racial pride as well as gender awareness in imagining what was possible for Black people. As it emerged in the last decade of the nineteenth century and extended into the 1940s, New Negro Womanhood was a movement of self-determination for and by Black women that refused the "socially contingent" starting point of respectability.[15] New Negro Womanhood attracted Black women from varied life stations and included many of the race women of the Progressive Era who articulated early critiques of whiteness and patriarchy. Believing in their "inherent dignity," New Negro Women founded the first Black college sororities, encouraged the promotion of summer camps for Black girls, helped sustain liberating recreational spaces, and created schools specifically for working-class Black girls.[16] Each of these interventions established humanizing geographies in which Black girls and women were able to inhabit fuller and more empowered versions of themselves. Within the framework of New Negro Womanhood, the Women's Dinner and much of Slowe's work on behalf of Black college women becomes immediately intelligible.[17] That is, New Negro Womanhood was the racialized gender project at the base of her efforts to have Howard women live more abundantly.

The Women's Dinner—and the architecture and programming that came to constitute Howard University's Women's Campus—encouraged what Slowe termed the New Howard Woman, a New Negro Woman subject who resisted external definitions of self and approached the world as an equal to members of other race-gender groups. This book's cover photo captures aspects of this *femininity*, a term that I, like many feminist scholars, use as a synonym for *womanhood* to emphasize that "woman" is a socially constructed category. Taken in the 1930s by the Black-owned Scurlock Studio of Washington, D.C., the image depicts Slowe with about 150 Howard undergraduate women. They were probably members of the Women's League, an umbrella organization to which all women students belonged and that would sponsor the Women's Dinner. Standing closely in long rows on the steps of the university's Carnegie Building, the women are dressed in wide-lapeled and fur-collared winter coats that reach midcalf. Some students sport close-fitting slouch hats worn at a fashionable tilt. Several hold books in the crooks of their arms. Slightly off center in the first row is Slowe, and a student standing to the dean's left angles her upper body toward the administrator. As they collectively look directly into the camera, the women exude focus and determination. Together, the dean and "her girls" make an impressive show of solidarity and pride as New Howard Women.

Sources

During her career Slowe realized a kind of education not already in existence for Black college women. In charting Slowe's philosophy, I drew heavily from her extensive papers—memos, articles, annual reports, letters, and photos—housed at Howard University's Moorland-Spingarn Research Center. These documents capture her educational vision and provide windows into how she promoted the rights of the New Howard Woman against the circumscribed recognitions extended to Black college women by white women deans and powerful men in the Howard University administrative hierarchy. I further situate Slowe's vision of living more abundantly within the evidence of two contemporaneous news sources. In articles published in the university's then biweekly student campus newspaper, the *Hilltop*, women students discussed the dean and her programming. The Baltimore-based *Afro-American* and other papers also covered her efforts.[18] Taken together, these public texts document the extent of support Slowe experienced from Howard women students, staff, and alumnae, as well as the resistance she faced to her premise that Black college women mattered.

Outside these archival sources, insights from a small but growing secondary literature about Slowe's character, career, and educational philosophy inform my work.[19] Foremost among these is the 2012 biography *Faithful to the Task at Hand: The Life of Lucy Diggs Slowe*, by Carroll L. L. Miller and Anne S. Pruitt-Logan. The product of an intergenerational effort undertaken by several individuals who had either studied with Slowe or been shaped by her teachings, *Faithful to the Task at Hand* details her half-century of existence, including her girlhood, early career as a high school teacher and administrator, and her fifteen years as the dean of women at her alma mater.[20] In its attention to the full arc of her life, *Faithful to the Task at Hand* supplements its analyses of archival material and news stories with a precious resource—interviews of former students and colleagues. Those familiar with the biography will recognize my indebtedness to it. However, in focusing on Slowe's years as dean at Howard, *To Live More Abundantly* elevates her intentional New Negro Woman philosophy and situates her ideology among early twentieth-century discourses of modern personhood. Specifically, it highlights how Slowe's vision of a racially and gender-inclusive democracy rested upon the connections she saw between higher education and contemporaneous movements toward self-determination.

My study reveals the depth of Slowe's investments in New Negro Womanhood for Howard women as well as the challenges she faced in upholding its principles among her Black men and white women peers. I examine her vision as it affected three spaces of her professional life: the women-centered extracurricular environment Slowe created on Howard University's campus, the white women–dominated field of deaning, and the heteropatriarchal administration of Howard University. In characterizing the New Howard Woman as a New Negro Woman, I also draw on a growing body of Black feminist scholarship that has challenged the "intersectional erasure" of Black women's experiences and voices within Black cultural institutions.[21] Particularly noteworthy in this literature are the pioneering insights of the historian Treva Lindsey, who first conceptualized Slowe as a New Negro Woman.[22] Lindsey attends to an important but underexplored movement of Black women's agency that pushed against the silences and accommodations prescribed by racial respectability. By detailing Slowe's campus efforts and her interactions with other administrators during her career as a New Negro Woman, my work extends Lindsey's analysis. Given the resonance between the New Howard Woman ideal and the aspirations and self-regard of generations of Howard undergraduates and alumnae, my work participates in the recovery of gender histories that fall outside the heteronormative "racial manhood" that is the typical focus of institutional accounts of HBCUs.[23]

A Road Map

Chapter 1, "Refusing Respectabilities: The New Negro Woman," discusses the novelty and boldness, given the currency of respectability in Black institutions as well as in the wider white society, of an educational philosophy that encouraged Black women to live more abundantly. Slowe's outlook, however, derived from her participation in two contemporaneous interventions into sexist social dynamics. Specifically, the New Woman and the New Negro Woman identity movements supported her challenge to many of the educational structures that regarded Black women's minds and bodies as deficient and expendable.

Populated from the ranks of the first two generations of white alumnae (1870–1910), New Womanhood encouraged this demographic to develop their identities and proficiencies beyond their relationships as wives, mothers, and daughters to white men. Amid their pathbreaking forays into white men's professions and their founding of the fields of social work, public health nursing, and early childhood education, New Women also established deaning in the early twentieth century to secure and extend white women's access to the opportunities of higher education. Too often forgotten as the foremothers of contemporary student affairs professionals, deans of women were the first administrators to insist on the extracurriculum as a critical space for students' development. Despite these deans' broadened view of college as a time for academic as well as social growth, they operated largely within New Women's racial boundaries and resisted seeing women of color as equals. Throughout her career Slowe challenged the field's predominant and singular focus on gender, because it failed to recognize her as a peer and thwarted her efforts to work collaboratively with white colleagues in support of Black college women.

More useful to Slowe in her advocacy of living more abundantly was the discourse of New Negro Womanhood. New Negro Women affirmed Black women's self-direction and equal standing and did not define themselves by the experience of slavery or take up a belief in their lesser status relative to other race-gender groups. As New Negro Women rejected the notions of Black femininity upheld by racial respectability, they insisted that Black communities and the wider society recognize and dismantle norms that maintained both white prerogative and men's privilege. Advancing a progressive and feminist Black womanhood, several New Negro Women were Slowe's contemporaries and noteworthy educators in Washington, D.C. As this first chapter highlights the affinities between the educational outlooks and efforts of the school leaders Anna Julia Cooper and Nannie Helen Burroughs, it provides a broader ideological context for the work Slowe undertook at Howard University. The chapter also demonstrates how Slowe and other New Negro Women openly rejected the entrenched heteropatriarchal "gender silence" within Black communities and institutions.[24]

During her tenure Slowe worked with her small staff and Howard's women students to promote several material and cultural campus changes aligned with the emergent deaning movement: she introduced the Women's Dinner, lobbied successfully for the building of three state-of-the-art dormitories, and supported a range of extracurricular leadership, social, and athletic opportunities for Howard's women students. To intervene more broadly against the minimization of young Black women's potential throughout Black-serving colleges and universities, Slowe founded two higher education advocacy organizations: the National Association of College Women in (NACW) 1923, and the National Association of Women's Deans and Advisers of Colored Schools (NAWDACS) in 1929. Furthermore, as the first Black dean of women in the United States, Slowe gave speeches and authored articles on Black college women's educational needs. Drawing on these materials, in chapter 2, "We Are the New Howard Woman: Educating a Modern Black Femininity," I examine Slowe's efforts to transform Howard University into a gender-inclusive institution. The chapter also documents how students took up her invitation to become New Howard Women. As undergraduate women revealed in their accounts of Slowe's efforts published in the *Hilltop*, the New Howard Woman resonated deeply with students, who largely partnered with Slowe in establishing a women-centered extracurriculum.

Holmes's complete statement in his eulogy from which I take Slowe's philosophy, reads, "She gave the last full measure of devotion that girls, all girls, might live more abundantly." The purposeful emphasis of "girls, all girls" recognized that while Slowe's work was grounded in deaning, the profession's conceptualization of young womanhood excluded her girls, Black college women. Slowe belonged to two majority white New Women organizations involved in higher education and advocacy for women—the Young Women's Christian Association (YWCA) and the National Association of Deans of Women (NADW). Although both struggled to become racially inclusive, the YWCA's religious grounding and social gospel orientation rendered it far more responsive to fostering interracial cooperation than the secular NADW, which exhibited much racial evasiveness and resistance to the full incorporation of Slowe and the Black deans who followed her path-forging lead. Chapter 3, "Race Work Is Women's Work: Deaning and the Color Line," holds a mirror up to the shared purpose and sisterhood claimed by both organizations. In it I examine instances of white women's indifference and highlight the actions of some who worked against the anti-Black color line evident in higher education and in the associations of the New Women deans. As Slowe confronted the racial arrogance of white women, she held to a central principle, which was evident in her talks, memos, and private letters to her peers: interracial work was, in fact, the work of all women.

Although the frame of respectability predominated in evaluations of Black women throughout society, by the time Slowe joined the administration of Howard University, she and other Black women found themselves devalued by another discourse of Black personhood—the New Negro. Rather than advancing the deference to whites that respectability expected, the New Negro promoted assertiveness and self-determination but largely envisioned these qualities as the prerogatives of Black men. Like "the regime of respectability," then, the rise of New Negro manhood subordinated Black women within a gender order that compromised their agency, growth, and leadership.[25]

Most of Slowe's career as dean took place during the administration of Howard University's first African American president, Mordecai Wyatt Johnson, whose tenure stretched from 1926 to 1960. Despite raising the university's stature and modernizing its offerings, Johnson's New Negro approach to the higher education of Black women actively resisted Slowe's New Negro Women assertions of equality and partnership. As her deaning efforts gained traction on Howard's campus and she acquired national visibility, Johnson and the board of trustees used the university's governing structures to target her for humiliation and professional diminishment. In chapter 4, "Our Dean, Our Selves: The Persecution and Defense of a New Negro Woman," I focus on this decadelong clash between Slowe's philosophy of growth for Black women and the paternalism of the Johnson administration. Throughout this period Slowe received ongoing support from Howard's women students, its alumnae, and the Black press; in fact, many attributed her death at age fifty-four to this protracted harassment. The public nature of both Slowe's mistreatment and the resistance that welled up against it—particularly among women students—reveal that Slowe was far from alone in her advocacy of New Negro womanhood within the structures of Howard University.

Although her early death was an enormous loss to Howard women and the profession of deaning, it is important to remember Slowe's original vision of living more abundantly. The conclusion, "Remembering Dean

Lucy Diggs Slowe," considers the many ways Howard women understood her legacy and sought to preserve it, intentionally defying the race loyalty norms that usually silenced Black women's experiences of patriarchal harm. This final chapter gives voice to her supporters, including her life partner, Mary Burrill; selected Howard University colleagues; and Howard alumnae. They carried forward her vision in letters of condolence, appeals for recognition in the Black press, and the maintenance of traditions explicitly tied to championing the New Howard Woman. Perhaps the greatest testament to her influence is that Howard women continued the Women's Dinner for three decades after her passing.

To pioneer is to forge new worlds and needed pathways, to stand alone at moments but on behalf of many others, and to walk with "a belief in self far greater than anyone's disbelief."[26] As a New Negro Woman and as a dean of women, Lucy Diggs Slowe operationalized her conviction that Black college women were relevant figures in higher education and society. For those of us interested in the ongoing project of inclusion, Slowe is a foremother whose vision and struggles to honor the promise of young Black women can illuminate our own.

REFUSING RESPECTABILITIES
THE NEW NEGRO WOMAN

> Education must fit Negro women, as it must fit all women, for the
> highest development of their own gifts; but, whatever those gifts, they
> will not be able to exercise them unless they understand the world
> they live in and are prepared to make their contribution to it.
>
> **Lucy Diggs Slowe, "Higher Education of Negro Women," July 1933**

When Lucy Diggs Slowe returned to her alma mater in 1922 as its first
full-time dean of women, Howard University was known as the "Negroes'
Harvard."[1] It was the flagship institution within a system of public and private, black- and white-founded colleges and universities that largely came
into existence after the Civil War. Collectively known as historically black
colleges and universities (HBCUs), these institutions had to contend with
not only systemic underfunding but also white concerns about the role that
African Americans could and should play in U.S. society. In a kind of racial
compromise, a majority of the 121 public and private HBCUs that existed in
1930 engaged in some form of "respectability training," which resulted in
what LaKisha Simmons terms a "dual education—instruction in academic
subjects and respectability."[2] Such a moralistic focus in the curriculum un-
dergirded the peer advice offered in the 1920s by women students at Spel-
man College. Conceding that they would always encounter harshly evaluative audiences, the authors stressed the importance of Black women's
monitoring their behavior "not for ourselves alone but for the sake of less-
ening conflict with others whom we meet."[3] Thus, whether motivated to
liberate or rehabilitate a formerly enslaved population, such institutions of-

ten focused their efforts less on questioning white norms than on preparing Blacks to accommodate themselves to those social expectations.

By 1922, when Slowe became Howard's first full-time dean of women, the effect of such strictures of respectability were evident in Black women's educational access and postgraduate trajectories. Collectively, the race was underrepresented in higher education. In the first decades of the post-Emancipation era, Black men were more likely than Black women to attend and complete college. However, beginning in the 1920s, Black women began to claim a larger percentage of the undergraduate degrees among African Americans. By 1930, when Blacks constituted about 10 percent of the U.S. population and accounted for only 1.8 percent of all the bachelor's degrees granted, Black women garnered 2 percent of the degrees awarded to women, while Black men secured only 1.6 percent of the bachelor's degrees earned by U.S. men. A decade later, in 1940, Black women merited more than half (56.8 percent) of all degrees conferred by HBCUs.[4]

Black women's apparent advantage in degree completion relative to Black men reflected a community-supported and personally protective strategy of "socially responsible individualism." Black families encouraged young women to attend college to prepare for the teaching profession, both to contribute to the actual educational needs of the community and, as important, to evade their concentration in the economically and physically exploitative fields of domestic service and agriculture.[5] In 1930 these two sectors employed 78.2 percent of working Black women, while only 3.4 percent of Black women wage earners were engaged in professional and technical labor, typically as teachers. Among white women in the labor force, 16.1 percent earned wages through agriculture and household service, while a full quarter (25.3 percent) were remunerated for professional and technical work.[6]

Throughout the first half of the twentieth century, more than 80 percent of Black alumnae took up the respectable and feminized work of teaching within Black segregated schools. The high percentage reflected the severe limitations of the job market for women of color, the association of Black feminine goodness with social service, and the devaluation of women's leadership in Black men's own bids for first-class citizenship.[7] Given codes of racial respectability, education for self-fulfillment or personal development was deemed "more a luxury than a necessity" for Black women.[8]

REFUSING RESPECTABILITIES

To disrupt and shift these patterns of educational containment that were well established for Black women in communities and institutions aligned with racial respectability, Slowe drew on two movements for self-determination: the New Woman and the New Negro Woman. While the first grounded her professional focus on Howard women's extracurricular lives and development, the second fostered her convictions about the inherent value of Black women. Combined, they nurtured and affirmed her radical attention to Black collegiate womanhood.

The New Woman
Pursuing Education for Individual Growth
and Social Usefulness

The end of the Civil War brought measured educational opportunity to Blacks but much more to white women. To compensate for reversals of fortune and the loss of young white men, a number of colleges and universities founded exclusively for this demographic pragmatically but reluctantly engaged in coeducation. This so-called experiment of granting white women access—often limited and highly regulated—to the dominion of higher education soon became a financially expedient strategy for spurring institutional growth. Admitting women also provided a means for meeting increasing social pressure—particularly at state-funded public institutions—for more democratic access to institutions of higher education.[9]

The half-century between 1870 and 1920 was transformative for white women in higher education. Whereas in 1870 more than half of colleges were for men only (59 percent), by the turn of the century 70 percent of institutions were coeducational.[10] During this period of increased access, the percentage of college women grew tenfold, from 0.7 percent of all young women aged eighteen to twenty-one to 7.6 percent of this demographic. Furthermore, although white women constituted 21 percent of college and university students in 1879, by 1920 they accounted for almost half (47.3 percent) of all enrolled undergraduates.[11] Amid this expansion of their presence, white college women forged a new identity for themselves—the New Woman.

Despite social anxiety about the consequences of their entrance into an historically masculine sphere, the first two generations of alumnae (1870–90 and 1890–1910)—at both single sex and coeducational institutions—

excelled academically and countered doubts about their physical and intellectual abilities to pursue courses of study that had been restricted to men.[12] As one early Wellesley College alumna recalled, "We were pioneers in the adventure,—voyagers in the crusade for the higher education of women,—that perilous experiment of the [18]70's, which all the world was breathlessly watching and which the prophets were declaring to be so inevitably fatal to the American girl."[13] Drawing heavily from the experiences of these mission-driven alumnae, New Women sought a "symmetrical," rather than a dependent, relationship to white men.[14] Because advocates of New Womanhood asserted that women had "two sides—the woman side, and the human side," they contended that "education was a right of personality rather than of sex."[15] They further maintained that the development of their latter qualities would render educated white women "well-equipped member[s] of a modern democratic community."[16] New Women's recognition of careers and employment as viable and worthy life options reflected their insistence on a fundamental equality with white men as "soul[s] born to immortality."[17]

Only about half the members of the first two generations of white alumnae married, unlike 90 percent of their non-college-educated peers.[18] Such low rates of matrimony poignantly—and, to some social observers, disturbingly—demonstrated the power of higher education to expand conceptions of women's place and shift their life trajectories. For many of these New Women, their choices to work and live in homosocial circles constituted an intentional revolt against the constraints of patriarchal social organization, within marriage and motherhood as well as throughout other social institutions.[19] New Women became pioneers in men's occupations, political activists, and founders of new Progressive Era movements—including settlement houses, public health nursing, early childhood education, and pacifism—out of their studied resistance to a domination ethos that pervaded society's norms and structures.[20]

Higher education's centrality to fostering a New Woman consciousness also accounts for the racial exclusivity of this early twentieth-century feminism. From the Civil War through the civil rights movement, most of higher education supported white dominance and intentionally matriculated only token numbers of Black women. To illuminate the pointed resistance of the elite New England women's colleges to admitting Black women students, the historian Linda Perkins compared their enrollment numbers to those of Oberlin College. Unlike most other higher education institutions founded before the Civil War, Oberlin opened in 1833 with a commitment to "interracial coeducation."[21] As a result, it offered access to people of color and women, and during its first eighty years, the college matriculated more than four hundred African American women. From 1890 to 1960, the seven elite women's colleges collectively awarded degrees to only five hundred Black women, at an average rate of one per year per institution. In actuality, however, the Seven Sisters' receptiveness to racially diverse women varied widely: although some admitted one or two annually early in their founding in the late nineteenth century, others barred Black women from their campuses until well into the twentieth century.[22]

Bryn Mawr College's president, M. Carey Thomas, a pioneer in higher education, espoused white racial domination and explicitly connected it to white women's educational opportunity. During an opening convocation in 1916, Thomas proclaimed to her campus audience, "If the present intellectual supremacy of the White races is maintained, as I hope that it will be for centuries to come, I believe it will be because they are the only races that have seriously begun to educate their women." As she expressed xenophobic concerns about the immigration of "the backward people of Europe like the Czechs, the Slavs, and the south Italians," Thomas also denigrated "the pure negroes of Africa, the Indians, the Esquimaux, the South Sea Islanders, the Turks, etc" for failing to demonstrate any "continuous mental activity." Given her focus on maintaining a student body largely descended from "early time Americans," Thomas blocked the admission of Black women during her twenty-eight-year tenure as president, from 1894 to 1922.[23]

Despite Thomas's racist limitation of New Womanhood ideals of self-definition and social leadership to white upper-class women, this movement actually appealed to women around the world and from diverse cultural and racial backgrounds within the United States.[24] However, in its hegemonic understandings, New Womanhood rested upon notions of whiteness and fears of racial mixing. Unsurprisingly, these attitudes were also constituent elements of New Women's founding of the profession to which Slowe belonged—deans of women.

New Women in Higher Education
Deans of Women

In 1920, despite approaching numerical parity with men, white women college students remained an unequal group in higher education, and their presence elicited much administrative ambivalence.[25] Discouraged by faculty and men students from fields deemed inconsistent with conventionally feminine qualities and life pursuits, these young women had, at best, limited access to extracurricular student activities—such as the newspaper, athletic teams, and student government—that developed leadership skills and built a sense of community among peers.[26] Institutional efforts to contain women in ways that were "compatible with their femininity" reflected a tacit policy of opposition to coeducation.[27] That is, despite white women's growing numbers and the critical revenue they contributed to the colleges and universities they attended, these students still attended campuses where expectations about their deference to men prevailed. In an effort to supervise young women's social and academic lives and align their aspirations with patriarchal gender norms, by the 1920s more than 90 percent of historically white colleges and universities had hired deans of women.[28]

Deans of women were the first women administrative leaders on coeducational campuses. As the largely unrecognized founders of the field of student affairs, they are also the foremothers of today's women's center directors and women's studies faculty.[29] In her attempt to retrieve these women from oblivion, the historian Carolyn Terry Bashaw describes their pioneering vision as "the best-kept secret in the history of higher education."[30] Although hired to supervise the residential lives of women students, the deans quickly organized into a self-defining profession. In 1916 they founded the National Association of Deans of Women (NADW), and in the same year Teachers College of Columbia University began offering graduate courses in the field.[31]

With the development of a scholarly literature, professional training, and annual conferences, deans of women began the work of establishing their administrative identity and genealogy. Tellingly, the NADW did not draw inspiration from the brief history of matrons, the middle-aged women who were hired by some mid-nineteenth-century college presidents to monitor the morals and residential lives of the few women students they had reluctantly admitted. Rather, for the NADW and its members, deaning came into being with the much more recent naming, in 1892, of Alice Freeman Palmer to the position at the newly founded University of Chicago.

At the time of her recruitment, Palmer was already an experienced administrative leader. A University of Michigan alumna and a Wellesley professor who became the college's president (1881–87), Palmer knew coeducation in its early contested years as well as the "Adamless Eden" of many white women's colleges.[32] With good reason she did not undertake the work of a dean as a subordinate but saw herself as a vice president for women students. Rather than defer to the campus president, she appealed to her own discretion "to tell him as little as I can, and take every bit of responsibility I dare assume."[33] Her approach resonated broadly with subsequent deans of women, who understood that without their presence and commitments to women students, colleges and universities would "continue to be in the future as the vast majority have been in the past,—institutions for men."[34]

Despite the calculation that deans of women would uphold and oversee a containment project in higher education, these administrative pioneers operated much more subversively. As alumnae who had experienced the liberating effect of college on their life cycle, deans of women worked with—but often stood at a critical distance from—the paternalistic visions of campus presidents, college men, and young women's families of origin.[35] Advocacy rather than surveillance was key to their efforts to press campuses for "women's share of space, prestige, and resources."[36]

During their own undergraduate years, the women who became deans of women had created extracurricular supports for themselves out of necessity. However, as professionals they found themselves facing a new problem. Between the two world wars, cohorts of more affluent and less academically focused undergraduate women encountered a well-established campus life organized around men's interests and prerogatives. Unlike the first two generations of college women, who were conscious of their contested presence as outsiders "treading on male turf," many white women in the first decades of the twentieth century matriculated matter-of-factly as "an act of conformity" with cultural norms and parental desires.[37] Amid the sororities, fraternity dances, smoking, movies, conspicuous consumption, weekend automobile trips, dancing, dating, and petting that made heterosociability the norm, young white women approached college as a culturally sanctioned stepping-stone to a good marriage.[38]

To counter institutional imperatives attempting to consign women to a "'second class' relationship" relative to men, deans of women championed the development of students as multidimensional people and not simply as intellectual beings.[39] The deans argued for the existence and interdependence of two curricula in higher education—the academic and the social. Better known and highly valued, the academic curriculum was directed by faculty and managed through adult authority. As important as it was for the transfer of cultural knowledge, it fell short of what deans of women asserted was also needed—opportunities for students to put into action the lessons in character they were learning in the classroom. Students organized the social curriculum and were advised by administrators, such as deans of women, who saw deep value in democratic living and the "socially broadening" opportunities of student-led government, organizations, clubs, housing associations, unions, lounges, and offices.[40] Thyrsa Amos, dean of women at the University of Pittsburgh, explained the interdependence of both forms of preparation for a holistic education: "If the academic curriculum trains to think and to know, and the social trains to contact and to work successfully with people, what greater worth can be hoped for in education?"[41] Deans of women faulted as problematic a curriculum unduly focused on subject matter because it led faculty to "forget that they are not teaching subjects" but students whose overall development was the focus of the undergraduate experience.[42]

Deans of women declared themselves experts in women's education because they were "the only officer in the university who deals with a woman student as a complete human being."[43] Given this understanding of their role, they insisted on the need for three distinct campus environments—"that for men alone, that for women alone, and that for men and women together."[44] Taking a developmental approach to students, deans of women viewed the college years as critical in setting the life course of young women, and they staunchly refused to "tak[e] the low road of cultural accommodation and stereotypical behavior—house the women, protect them from the men, prepare them for marriage."[45] As expressed by Lois Mathews Rosenberry, dean of women at the University of Wisconsin, in her 1915 profession-defining text, *The Dean of Women*, the goal of higher education was to broaden women's horizons, not dictate a particular future for them: "If a young woman has during her university career been made aware, both inside the classroom and outside of the college community, of her inescapable obligation to bring her trained mind and unselfish spirit to bear upon questions of human welfare wherever she may meet them, she cannot fail to take her place and contribute her share to the world's work."[46] Like many of her colleagues, Rosenberry acknowledged traditional life paths, such as marriage and motherhood, while consistently and defiantly committing to expanding young women's reputable efforts to include work in an "independent career," which could take form in the federal civil service, nursing, and social settlements, as well as law and medicine.[47]

Strategically, deans of women nodded to feminine conventions, but, more important, they staunchly insisted on young women's right to develop well beyond these gendered limitations. The deans were engaged in cultivating a new kind of adult woman, who "possess[ed] the virtues of strength, of courage, of initiative, of ability to fend for themselves, of honestly facing the problems of living and of assuming full responsibility for doing their share in the world's work." The twentieth century, they argued, would not be well served by encouraging an outdated, "sentimental, dependent type" of womanhood.[48] As they promoted notions of white women's possibility that were not narrowly limited to domesticity, deans of women were preparing college women to be active citizens able to shape "a new social order."[49] In the words of Sarah Sturtevant, a professor at Teachers College, the profession of deaning sought not to accommodate women to men-administered campuses or sexist social attitudes but to help women "blaze the way" to an improved, democratic society.[50]

As the deans established traditions of mentoring, campus programming, and self-governance for students, some of these administrators directly encouraged playfulness among college women. Dean Amos helped found the Women's Athletic Association, the student body that went on to sponsor an annual Co-ed Prom to recruit new students to campus athletics at the University of Pittsburgh. From 1922 to 1937 juniors and seniors dressed as men and accompanied their dates, femininely attired women students who were first-years and transfers. With obvious delight a 1932 article in the university newspaper detailed how the "unusual couples" in attendance appropriated and contested heteropatriarchal norms: "Tuxedoed upperclasswomen escort[ed] rompered, bubbling freshmen. Plump little girls and 'boys' sucked giant lollypops; uniformed heroes chatted with dainty maids, and 'football players' with grotesquely expansive chests and shoul-

Co-ed Prom, 1936. University of Pittsburgh.
Archives & Special Collections, University of Pittsburgh Library System.

ders cavorted among the dancers. Tall 'kiddies' danced with tiny 'gentle-men.'"[51] During the sixteen years of the prom's existence, Amos supported the efforts of these college women to stretch and mock narrowly conventional beliefs about who they were and what they could do.[52]

Such gender irreverence is almost unrecognizable in the cultural imagery that arose about deans of women, who are represented as prudish older women attempting to thwart young people's social lives.[53] Although the deans strongly eschewed some modern aspects of youth culture—which one dean described as "the vices and bad habits of smoking and drinking, of using coarse and common language, of indifference to the niceties of living"—most understood concerns about coeducation as centering much less on women's propriety than on what Slowe herself pointedly identified as "essentially the problem of educating 'the weaker sex' in colleges with 'the stronger sex.'"[54] Standing at a critical distance from the paternalistic visions of campus presidents and faculty, college men, and young women's families, deans of women pursued their work of shifting gender norms and campus structures.[55] Their goal was to create conditions that would allow young women to graduate with the self-knowledge and practical skills needed for making informed choices about their futures.

The Demise of the Profession of Deans of Women

The attention of deans of women to the extracurricular needs of women students ushered in the office of deans of men, avuncular administrators who loosely curbed the excesses of a youthful and privileged white masculinity.[56] Deans of men undertook little of the gender challenge that defined the work of deans of women, who guided the development of clubs, programming, and physical space for women against institutional resistance. To put it bluntly, while deans of women were invested in cultural change, deans of men largely did not question the norms of masculine dominance on college campuses.

By the 1960s most coeducational colleges and universities had consolidated the roles of deans of women and men into an office of "student affairs." In a turn away from a policy of gender separation and out of concern about rising student social activism on campuses, this restructuring was devastating to many women deans.[57] Operating with sexist assumptions about leadership ability, coeducational colleges typically promoted deans of men to a cabinet-level role while demoting deans of women—even when they outranked such men or had more professional experience—within the administrative structure. As a result, whereas in 1936, 86 percent of deans of women reported directly to their university's president, by 1963 fewer than a third (29.5 percent) had such access.[58] Although this reorganization ended the tenures of deans of women on coeducational campuses, a number of women's colleges recognized these administrators' skill and experience with gender advocacy and recruited them for presidencies.[59]

As the first women in higher education administration, deans of women innovated a responsive extracurriculum to support young women's exploration of selfhood outside an institutionalized subordination to men. The women deans understood that, despite the presence of women students, most institutions remained centered on college men; these new administrators keenly believed in "the need for a leader of women in a co-educational college."[60] However, because the profession was founded within a particular demographic of New Women, deaning limited its notions of a modern femininity to white middle-class women. As a result, the major agents in deaning maintained and reinforced white dominance, failing to conceptualize educated womanhood in ways inclusive of racially minoritized women.

Refusing Respectabilities
New Negro Womanhood

Neither racial respectability nor the New Woman discourse spoke adequately to Dean Slowe's aspirations for Black women to have opportunities as full members of their campuses and society. Her extension of personal agency to educated Black women was therefore a radical act of social defiance. In this resistance Slowe drew on a lesser-known identity movement, New Negro Womanhood. Departing from the domesticity and men-centered racial uplift that respectability discourse put forward, New Negro Women dared to see self-actualization as a fundamental twentieth-century human right rather than a privilege restricted to whites and men. In short, New Negro Women rejected forms of control and diminishment at odds with their bids for self-definition and self-determination.

Overlapping with the respectability discourse of the late nineteenth century and contemporaneous with the rise of New Women, New Negro Womanhood attracted a cross-class group of Black women, including college alumnae and professionals as well as self-employed beauticians, domestics, blues singers, entrepreneurs, and activists.[61] New Negro Women believed in their inalienable right to be consequential members of society and resisted what Kristie Dotson terms "epistemic backgrounding," or the ways the particular realities of Black women are typically devalued and overlooked within men-centered experiences of racism or white-focused definitions of womanhood.[62] In their rejection of forms of secondary and tertiary citizenship, New Negro Women insisted on the importance of their "self-discovery, self-acceptance, and self-fulfillment."[63]

The contemporary Black feminist scholars Treva Lindsey and Brittney Cooper locate the emergence of the New Negro Woman ethos at the 1893 World's Columbian Exposition in Chicago.[64] During the week of May 15 to May 22, six Black women activists challenged their exclusion from the World's Congress of Representative Women. In this international venue celebrating modernity and attracting five hundred speakers from twenty-seven countries, Frances E. W. Harper, Fannie Barrier Williams, Anna Julia Cooper, Fannie Jackson Coppin, Sarah J. Early, and

Hallie Q. Brown made some of the first public statements that established a "black-women-centered counternarrative" to their representation in white-dominated public life and community spaces controlled by men.[65] Unlike women who abided by the self-management codes and surveillance of respectability, New Negro Women pursued social critique. From these alternative understandings of self and society, they pressed for an articulation of value and place by Black women for Black women.

New Negro Women were guided not by feelings of shame regarding their race's condition but by a set of insistences: Black people were human beings, Black women had essential value, and the United States was structurally at fault for engaging in dominance rather than democracy in its interactions with large sectors of its populace. These Black women also believed that the dawn of a new century offered the possibility of a renegotiation of the social contract between different race-gender groups in the promotion of the American values of liberty and opportunity for all. As New Negro women focused on individual capacity and social contribution, they advanced a vision of an inclusive modern America—a democratic society no longer contorted under the twin pressures of white dominance and patriarchal structures.[66] Although they were not blind to the obvious inequities that existed or oblivious to the active social resistance to such a race- and gender-aware vision of justice, New Negro Women did stake a moral claim: they believed that America could make good on its ideals and become in everyday practice what it was in name—a space of personal growth and social improvement.

Born into slavery in 1858, Anna Julia Cooper was an 1884 graduate of Oberlin College and a noteworthy proponent of a racially inclusive notion of womanhood. In 1892 she published *A Voice from the South*, a compilation of essays articulating her rejection of an accommodationist stance toward the attitudes of white supremacist patriarchy. A year later at the Columbian Exposition, she upheld a vision of Black womanhood that insistently departed from nineteenth-century forms of dominance and invisibility. In her speech she asserted, "We want, then, as toilers for the universal triumph of justice and human rights, to go to our homes from this Congress, demanding an entrance not through a gateway for ourselves, our race, our sex, or our sect, but [through] a grand highway for humanity. The colored woman feels that woman's cause is one and universal."[67] Cooper focused on subordinated groups—"every man and . . . every woman who has writhed silently under a mighty wrong"—and emphasized Black women's individuality and human qualities, not their traditional gendered obligations or racialized limitations. She asserted that Black women were intellectually equipped to be ethical actors in public life, and she believed their efforts and insights were essential for reconstructing society away from "the unnaturalness and injustice of all special favoritisms, whether of sex, race, country, or condition."[68]

Cooper and other New Negro Women at the Columbian Exposition rejected patriarchal and racist notions of respectability. In their bold acts of self-definition, they sought to be known as free citizens and did not locate their identities in slavery and subordination. Countering respectability discourses anchored in white racism and men's dominance, New Negro Women presented Black women as knowers, creators, and leaders. Three decades after slavery, the words of Fannie Barrier Williams (1855–1944), the educator, social commentator, and women's rights activist, conveyed the self-determination of New Negro Women and their prospective outlook toward a "new horizon" of social inclusion and contribution.[69] As she proclaimed, "We believe that the world always needs the influence of every good and capable woman, and this rule recognizes no exceptions based on complexion. . . . The contentions of colored women are in kind like those of other American women for greater freedom of development. Liberty to be all that we can be, without artificial hindrances, is a thing no less precious to us than to women generally."[70] New Negro Women believed that their independence and social contributions were assets to Blacks as well as women.[71]

Focusing her attention on the years after the Civil War, the Black suffragist and antislavery lecturer Frances E. W. Harper (1825–1911) approached the challenges of the early twentieth century with a sense of optimism and engaged purpose. Despite the "restlessness, religious upheavals, failures, blunders, and crimes" of the age, she viewed the arc of social change as bending toward "an increase of knowledge, the emancipation of thought, and a recognition of the brotherhood of man." Referring to the new century as the "woman's era," Harper considered women no longer as men's subordinates but rather as their companion and a sharer in such forward strides. Women had important social insights and, in distinction to men, were "grandly constructive" in their efforts and contributions.[72]

Williams and the other "self-emancipating" New Negro Women expected broad opportunities as collaborators in society.[73] Aware that they were "confronted by both a woman question and a race problem, and [were] as yet an unknown or an unacknowledged factor in both," New Negro Women considered their insights relevant to democratic praxis.[74] As Maude E. Brown, the international president of Alpha Kappa Alpha Sorority (AKA), expressed in 1938, "The college woman accepts the challenge to demand not segregation, but full and open competition. For, as a minority group, we want equal opportunity and equal protection under the law in our courts and out of them. We wish to be considered American."[75] New Negro Women would not abide by what Trimiko Melancon has termed "the classical black female script," which enforced men-defined notions of both race loyalty and femininity. Instead New Negro Women articulated and championed a consciously intersectional insistence on their social value.[76]

Of Women and Girls
New Negro Women and
Youthful Black Femininity

Significantly, New Negro Women were among the first to attend to the needs of Black girls and the developmental and social importance of Black girlhood. In 1905, twelve years after her address at the Columbian Exposition, the fifty-year-old Williams published "The Colored Girl," an essay in which she examined the particular problem of Black girl invisibility. Referencing W. E. B. Du Bois's 1903 concept of Black men's awareness of being perceived as a problem, Williams asserted that the colored girl managed an additional level of disregard because "she lives beneath the shadow of that problem which envelopes and obscures her." Given white racism as well as adult-centered and patriarchal understandings of Blackness, the Black girl was a cipher—a figure "not known and hence not believed in." Although the Black girl was overlooked even within her own community, Williams maintained that she was "like other girls in heart, brain and soul."[77]

In her social commentary, Williams both criticized whites and Black men for "hold[ing] our girls too cheaply" and emphasized what only a Black woman could envision and celebrate—that despite social obstacles and devaluations, Black girls were irrepressible. Exhibiting "enterprise and ambition that are always in advance of her opportunities," and drawing on these qualities, the colored girl was "pluckily challenging this humiliating color line." Williams described Black girls as essential social actors who were undaunted by the injustices they encountered. As Williams insisted, "We cannot comprehend the term American womanhood without including the colored girl." For her defiance of negative expectations and "demands [for] respect . . . the most interesting girl of this country is the colored girl."[78]

Anna Julia Cooper similarly focused on the neglected potential of Black girls. In "The Higher Education of Women," written in 1892, Cooper drew on her own experiences to expose how Black segregated communities invested disproportionately in boys' success. As a result, Cooper "constantly felt (as I suppose many an ambitious girl has felt) a thumping from within unanswered by any beckoning from without." Cooper argued against the view held among men—across race—that "the great law of self development was obligatory on their half of the human family only." She encouraged her audiences to uphold an equality of encouragement: no less than their boy counterparts, Black girls needed to know that the social need "for their trained, efficient forces" was great.[79]

New Negro Women's recognition of Black girls' individuality comports with Nazera Sadiq Wright's analysis of how social standing influenced literary treatments of Black girlhood throughout the nineteenth century. As Black men idealized Black girl figures to align with their own investments in a hardworking, devoted, and ultimately compliant adult Black womanhood, white authors wrote from a perch of racial superiority and presented Black girls as experiencing moral improvement and rehabilitation through contact with their social betters—that is, whites. In marked and important contrast, Black women writers drew the most textured representations of Black girls. As these writers "tended to focus on the interiority of the girls," they made visible a range of "thoughts . . . plans . . . dreams and aspirations." Williams and other Black women writers of the mid- to late nineteenth century depicted young Black women as "heroic and sensitive, quick-thinking and courageous."[80] These girls were both the developmental past and the social future of Black womanhood.

New Negro Women also worked to widen the professional horizons available to Black girls. In the 1920s AKA, the African American sorority

Slowe helped found at Howard University in 1908 and led in its inaugural year, introduced vocational education as its national philanthropy. AKA women organized career guidance weeks and clubs at high schools, and they raised scholarship money for young Black women to attend college.[81] AKA's outlook diverged from the respectability discourse that constrained black women's identities to being mother citizens and race mothers who would undertake work that did not threaten Black men's leadership prerogative. As New Negro Women, these sorors asserted that as much as their white peers, Black girls and women ought to determine the line of activity that would allow for powerful synergies between their personal strengths and societal needs.[82] Engaging in what they termed scientific, rather than simply moralistic or maternalistic, arguments about social progress, AKA women declared that "all girls had the potential to use professions [and not simply motherhood] to uplift the race."[83]

Slowe's contemporary, the African American educator Elise Johnson McDougald (1885–1971), understood the significance of this vocational support for its specific focus on Black women and not just the advancement of Black men. In her 1925 essay, "The Task of Negro Womanhood," McDougald recognized the work of a local AKA chapter that had provided "girls a chance to hear the life stories of Negro women, successful in various fields of endeavor."[84] Featured professions included trained nursing, commercial art, medicine and dentistry, and journalism. McDougald also noted the significant material support of a $1,000 scholarship for study abroad presented to an art major by a New York City chapter of the second Black sorority founded in the United States, Delta Sigma Theta. These efforts toward the vocational expansion of Black girls and young women were all the more striking to McDougald given that prevailing racialized constructions defined their primary work as helping Black men and boys "overcome the fatal, insidious inferiority complex" of slavery and segregation.[85]

Washington, D.C.
A City of New Negro Women

In the early decades of the twentieth century, Washington, D.C., was home to several prominent New Negro Women who founded schools. Significantly, these institutional leaders rejected deficit-driven philosophies and practices with regard to the education of Black girls and young women.[86] As such, their efforts resonated with Williams's championing of the potential of young Black women and girls.

Throughout her fifty-year career as a high school educator and administrator, Anna Julia Cooper staunchly promoted a liberal arts education, as well as young Black women's access to higher education and professions of their choice. During her principalship from 1901 to 1906 of M Street, the leading high school for African Americans in Washington, D.C., students earned admission to elite liberal arts institutions in the North and Midwest.[87] That girls comprised 80 percent of the students in her first year as principal and that women dominated the teaching staff likely rendered the school's success even more jarring to those opposed to Black women's social progress.[88] With Cooper's refusal to deliver an exclusively vocational curriculum, the white superintendent and African American men school board members demoted her from the leadership position.[89] In 1910, a subsequent board president recruited Cooper to return to M Street, where she remained a teacher of Latin, math, and science until 1930. Embodying the principle of lifelong learning, Cooper earned a doctoral degree from the Sorbonne in 1925, when she was sixty-six. During the first eleven years of her retirement, she assumed another leadership role, serving as the second president of the only extension school for working-class Blacks in the nation's capital, Frelinghuysen University. Evident in Cooper's life and career was her belief that education should serve the intertwined goals of "self-improvement and human betterment, as well as . . . social transformation."[90]

Washington, D.C., was also the location of Nannie Burroughs's National Training School for Women and Girls. A bold educational enterprise that focused on young Black women, the training school operated for more than a half-century, from 1909 to 1961. As a proud, dark-skinned, working-class African American woman, Burroughs challenged the ideologies and devaluations of white racism, bourgeois elitism, and Black chauvinism. She rejected the scorn for manual labor within both Black and white middle-class communities and professionalized forms of work to which the masses of Black women had access. The school's all-women, college-educated faculty attracted industrious girls and young women from throughout the United States, Caribbean, and Africa.[91] Burroughs explicitly acknowledged the gender project at the core of her institution:

"This school builds womanhood. . . . There is such a great need for young women of talent and leadership ability, who really want to let their lights shine in this 'confused' world, that we have highly resolved to find and train leaders."[92]

The National Training School's motto—"Work. Support thyself. To thine own powers appeal"—articulated a powerful set of expectations that prized Black women's capacity as "self-respecting wage earners" and community leaders.[93] Burroughs insisted on standards of excellence for Black women as a way to build their independence as workers who "if they cannot get what they would like to do . . . must like what they get to do, and do their work so efficiently that they will deserve and can demand something better."[94] The curriculum manifested her racial pride: mandatory courses in Black history and the liberal arts complemented the entrepreneurial spirit of the school as well as Burroughs's voiceful rejection of white notions of Black inferiority.[95]

Burroughs's vision of a school that focused on the particular needs and success of Black girls and young women was "the exception among African Americans at that time" and reflected her commitment to fostering Black women's autonomy from both racist and patriarchal constraints.[96] She attributed developmental value to single-gender schooling, stating, "Careful investigation shows that the women who are rendering the most effective service in slum, social settlement, reformatory and missionary work were trained in separate schools [from men]. The normal adolescent girl quickly 'finds herself' if she is given three or four years in a girls' school."[97] Burroughs saw Black girls and women as important, valuable, and skilled members of the labor market. And as she embraced the self-determination and assertiveness of New Negro Womanhood, Burroughs emphasized that, at her school, students and faculty "'specialize[d] in the wholly impossible.'"[98]

Lucy Diggs Slowe
A New Negro Woman

When Slowe began her tenure at Howard University in 1922, she was thirty-nine and had already charted a personal and professional path as a New Negro Woman. Born on July 4, 1883, in Berryville, Virginia, she was the youngest of five surviving children.[99] Her father, who owned the only

Lucy Diggs Slowe, fall 1922, her first term as dean at Howard.
Courtesy of the Moorland-Spingarn Research Center, Howard University Archives,
Howard University, Washington, D.C.

hotel in town, died when Slowe was nine months old. After her mother passed away five years later, a paternal aunt raised Slowe in Lexington, Virginia, and then Baltimore. As salutatorian of her 1904 class at what today is Frederick Douglass High School in Baltimore, Slowe earned a scholarship to attend Howard University and became the first young woman from her school to matriculate at this flagship institution of Black higher education.[100]

As an undergraduate Slowe majored in English, sang with the university choir, and presided over the Women's Tennis Club, all while working to finance her education.[101] With eight other Howard juniors and seniors, she cofounded the first African American women's Greek letter organization in the country, Alpha Kappa Alpha (AKA), and served as its inaugural president. Throughout her college career she demonstrated the kind of leadership and maturity she would later cultivate in her women students. As her oratory professor, Coralie Franklin Cook (1861–1942), recalled in a tribute after Slowe's death, the dean had approached her college years as "the time to make decisions, to adopt standards, to choose pathways—to build character. . . . She seemed instinctively a feminist."[102] In 1908 Slowe graduated at the top of her Howard University class of sixteen, which included equal numbers of women and men.[103]

After college Slowe became a well-regarded, innovative, and progressive educator. She returned to her high school, where she taught English and history for seven years, from 1908 to 1915.[104] In this early part of her teaching career, Slowe took graduate classes during the summer session at Columbia University, and in 1915 she earned her master's degree in English literature. Deaning took hold at colleges as well as high schools, and during Slowe's teaching tenure at Armstrong High School (1915–19) in Washington, D.C., she spent one year (1918–19) overseeing the welfare of girls.[105]

In 1919 Slowe's innovativeness led to her being recruited to serve as principal of the first junior high school for Black students in the capital, M Street Junior High, which was renamed for Robert Gould Shaw in 1921. Junior high schools were a new and "doubtful experiment" that had only recently (1909) been introduced to the American educational landscape.[106] These schools focused on the needs of early adolescents (ages ten to fifteen) and linked students' educational experiences to the social responsibilities of a democracy. As they empowered "youth [to] come of age, acting out new roles as maturing social beings," junior high schools operated as "not just a learning place, but also a growing place."[107]

While she was principal of M Street/Shaw Junior High, Slowe proved herself a visionary and dynamic leader. During her three-year tenure the student body grew more than tenfold, from forty to five hundred students. These young people encountered a developmentally responsive academic program as well as an impressive array of cocurricular opportunities to expand their skills and experiences. The school supported an orchestra, publication of the first review of a junior high school in the capital, a cafeteria guided by scientific food preparation, and a theatre program whose props were constructed by students. The school also sponsored regular gender-specific assemblies designed to place students in "close contact with successful men and women of both races for instruction and inspiration," sports for girls as well as boys, recitals featuring noted artists, and faculty meetings called to manage problems and keep teachers abreast of "modern educational movements."[108] As she oversaw the educational offerings of the school, Slowe insisted on her students' right to independence and self-determination. By standing apart from the reductive nineteenth-century ideals held for women and Blacks, Slowe encouraged these young people to begin, as one eighth-grader wrote in the school publication, "dreaming dreams of our future."[109]

As an administrator Slowe championed ongoing education for area teachers. Working through her Teachers College connections, she established a Columbia University Extension Center at Shaw Junior High in 1920. Under her direction the center offered an interracial group of district teachers the opportunity to earn university credit by attending courses led by visiting experts. More than three hundred local educators took part in this professional development program.[110]

Slowe both aspired to the ideal of racial integration and actively rejected the devaluations of white racism. In February 1922, during her last semester as principal, she was elected president of the newly formed Columbian Education Association of Washington, which Black teachers had established for themselves to contest the segregation of the local chapters of the National Education Association into Black and white groups.[111] Many recognized her educational advocacy and leadership, and as a general circulation daily in Washington, D.C., editorialized in its announcement of her acceptance of the offer to become Howard University's dean of women: "The departure of progressive educators of this type is a serious blow to the public school system of this city."[112]

In this period of establishing herself as a local educator, Slowe demonstrated a range of New Negro Women interests and was a visible proponent of Progressive causes. A member of the National Association for the Advancement of Colored People (NAACP) and former secretary of the Baltimore branch, Slowe publicly supported both women's suffrage and racial inclusion.[113] Additionally, for more than fifteen years after her graduation from Howard, she continued to play tennis competitively, and in a 1917 singles tournament hosted by the American Tennis Association, she became the first Black woman to win a national sports championship. She defended the title in 1921 and retired from tennis in 1924.[114]

Conclusion

New Negro Women repudiated the presumptions of inferiority used to confine Black girls and women to lesser worlds of living. Unlike Blacks who invested in respectability, New Negro Women sought to determine for themselves their identities and the places they would occupy in the world.[115] As a result, New Negro Women did not cede psychic space to the misrecognitions of other groups. Rather, they insisted on their self-definition in the face of the racist and patriarchal contempt directed at them. As dean, what Slowe termed the New Howard Woman was a collegiate version of the New Negro Woman. This figure, Slowe believed, deserved an education that would allow her to live more abundantly—with support and opportunities for growth. The next chapters trace how Slowe promoted New Negro Womanhood at Howard and within higher education.

CHAPTER 2

WE ARE THE NEW HOWARD WOMAN
EDUCATING A MODERN BLACK FEMININITY

There is a new force in Howard University that will bring help, inspiration, guidance, [and] culture into the life of the women here. Already a coveted view down the long avenue of time has revealed the New Howard Woman as she is conceived by Dean Lucy Slowe, the new force on the University faculty that must make itself felt far down through the future.

—Mamie Geraldine Neale, "The New Howard Woman," *Howard University Record,* **1922**

Just eight days into the fall term of 1922, Dean Slowe called together the women students of Howard University. For this October 10 meeting her goal was not only to introduce herself and her role but to share something more important—her bold vision of possibility, which she hoped would resonate with these young Black women. This ideal, her New Howard Woman, was "intellectually alert, physically alert, and of extreme culture and refinement."[1] As this figure was simultaneously modern, African American, and a woman, encouraging her presence and viability at Howard served Slowe's larger goal of bringing New Negro Woman energies to the campus.

Neale, the third-year student reporting on the meeting for the alumni magazine, conveyed great enthusiasm among her classmates about their expectations of the campus's new full-time dean of women. She characterized the dean's presence as ushering in "a new day" for the institution overall and referred to Slowe as "the answer to a spiritual need in the life of the women here."[2] Neale and her peers found Slowe's ideal liberating, and they eagerly gravitated toward the dean's innovative construction of a collegiate Black womanhood.

Subsequent sections of Neale's article addressed the depth and immediacy of students' embrace of the New Howard Woman. Although they were attending the institution celebrated as the "Capstone of Negro Education," women were not well served by Howard University's structure.[3] Neale explained that "a woman might seek the aid of any number of professors of the highest rank" for academic assistance but received little guidance in dealing with those "indefinable problems of etiquette, grace, culture."[4] Howard women's awareness of their unmet cocurricular needs was not new. Seven years earlier, in 1915, thirty-three students had unsuccessfully lobbied the administration for a dean of their own. However, unlike most institutions of higher education, Howard had appointed the first dean of men in 1917, five years before filling the position for women.[5]

On a campus that slighted women, Neale recognized that Slowe, the alumna-turned-administrator, both understood this neglect and was committed to creating institutional space for an education that was responsive to Howard women's lives both inside and outside the classroom. Neale concluded her assessment of the introductory meeting with this powerful vow: "We, the women of Howard University, welcome Dean Slowe with eager, open arms and consecrate ourselves to this sacred task of evolving the New Howard Woman." What this resounding endorsement revealed was that while the New Howard Woman was Slowe's term, its qualities were attractive to the women students. In other words, Slowe's gender project was a labor that Neale and her peers not only would support but had long desired for themselves.

Three days after calling the women together, Slowe held a second meeting, this time with the men students. In an address titled "What a Howard Man Ought to Be," she declared, "Young men, I came to do a job!" As part of her agenda she challenged them to become "Ideal Howard Men," individuals who would acquire both knowledge and "character, the proper attitude toward women, and the social graces." Particularly important to Slowe was that the men see the need for "a better social co-operation between the sexes" on the coeducational campus.[6] She understood that for her advocacy of women students to be successful, the men would need to reconsider their relationships to women and see them as peers rather than subordinates.

Howard University was founded in 1867, two years after the end of the Civil War. Through an effort that brought together the Missionary Society of the First Congregational Church of Washington, D.C., and a congressional charter, Howard began operations as an inclusive site of higher education.[7] With its doors "open to all persons without distinction of race, sex or former condition," it was originally envisioned as an institution for preparing ministers and teachers.[8] In a few years, however, the university's mission expanded to include liberal arts education and graduate programs. Given the entrenched racial segregation of higher education, during Slowe's tenure as dean the university counted among its faculty many of the key Black intellectuals, artists, and innovators of the early twentieth century, including the philosopher Alain Locke; historians Carter G. Woodson and Merze Tate; sociologists E. Franklin Frazier, Dwight O. W. Holmes, and Charles S. Johnson; chemist Percy Julian; mathematician and sociologist Kelly Miller; and activist and instructor of elocution Coralie Franklin Cook.

Despite Howard's prominence and necessity for college-aspiring Black students, the university carried forward the gender and racial structures of the nineteenth century that Slowe found to be regressive impediments to her work of encouraging Black women's "participatory belonging" in their communities as well as society at large.[9] At Howard as well as other HBCUs, respectability norms upheld not only white dominance but Black men's prerogative. Highly critical of this dynamic, Slowe focused on establishing new, resistive, women-centered traditions. To this end she introduced conversations and activities that would part from what she regarded as outdated respectabilities. As she made clear in her two early overtures to groups of students, Slowe sought to transform her alma mater into a learning-living environment supportive of a new Black community in which women and men would share the responsibilities of modern citizenship. A major vehicle for shifting the institution toward being a "Greater and Better Howard" was the establishment of the Women's Dinner.[10]

Within a month of her outreach to the students, Slowe organized the signature tradition of her tenure—the Women's Dinner. Like many of her white women peers, Slowe understood that incubating young women's alternative visions of themselves and their future in the twentieth century required the creation of women-centered educational geographies. Slowe had proposed the idea for the dinner just days before it took place, and she worked with "a corps of efficient and enthusiastic workers of students and alumnae" to plan it.[11] This organizing committee of thirty-one sent the

1940 Women's Dinner.
Courtesy of Scurlock Studio Records, Archives Center, National
Museum of American History, Smithsonian Institution.

spirited letter described in the introduction that informed the men of the
campus of the upcoming event for women only.[12] Held in the campus dining hall that had opened that fall, the Women's Dinner excluded all men
except waitstaff from attendance. The organizers confidently described the
dinner as "'a twentieth century wonder,' Howard women enjoying themselves without the company of the men'" and announced a new Black femininity not beholden to old gendered patterns of control, invisibility, and
subservience.[13] As a result, on the night of the dinner, the men were allowed to gather on the balcony at an appointed time to see for themselves
the emergence of the New Howard Woman.

A student reporter for the *Record* summarized the dinner's significance, writing, "The whole affair gave the women a new conception of
what it means to be a student or an alumna of Howard University. We
look forward with pleasure to the second annual Howard Women's Dinner and many other such affairs that must create and develop a new force
for a Greater and Better Howard."[14] Like Slowe, this undergraduate un-

derstood the dinner's role in broadening the university's focus beyond the men. Another article described the gathering of 250 women students, faculty, and alumnae as "brilliant in every aspect." At this intergenerational "meeting of youth and experience . . . alumnae threw off their cares and problems" and expressed themselves through cheers and campus songs. Despite the merriment, not lost on the women attendees was the dinner's "far deeper significance," which was to "help awaken a woman's consciousness which is one of the first steps toward the evolution of the 'New Howard Woman.'"[15] A tradition that sustained generations of Howard women, the dinner was held on the first Friday of November during Slowe's fifteen-year tenure and for thirty years after her death.

At a time and in a context in which Black women were expected to accept patriarchal norms, and be emotionally guarded and mindful of the gaze of others, the inaugural Women's Dinner was a striking act of collective self-assertion and relaxed self-expression. In the new "pleasure geography" created by the gathering, Black college women defined the place and scale of their own contributions in full view of the campus men, including the president and deans, who—in accordance with the women's letter to them—witnessed the event from the balcony.[16]

Rather than operate with invisibility, hypervisibility, or surveillance at their own event, these Black women were centered, confident, and eager to be seen on their own terms as New Negro Women. That the Record's article about the dinner incorporated Slowe's own phrase, "the New Howard Woman," reflected a degree of student alignment with her vision and work. The Women's Dinner was a purposeful event and a shared undertaking of Slowe, women faculty, alumnae, and current women students. As such it showcased a New Negro Woman pride in Black women and their efforts independent of men.

At the Second Annual Women's Dinner, Slowe's own address was titled "The Obligations of the College Woman to Society," and Neale reported that, with much anticipation from students, Slowe "struck again the note that she has so often sounded: that the ideal college woman is a woman whose body is strong and vigorous, whose mind is keen and alert, whose heart is trained."[17] Another indication of Slowe's influence on the young women and their collective embrace of a modern Black femininity was a March 1924 campus publication that highlighted her attendance at the annual conference of the National Association of Deans of Women and referred to her as "a true representative of Howard's womanhood."[18] Year after year, newspaper accounts documented student expressions of gratitude for Slowe. In their "thunderous applause" for the dean, they recognized her original vision, ongoing efforts, and words encouraging them to realize their possibilities.[19]

Throughout Slowe's tenure, voicefulness and spirit remained celebrated mainstays of the Women's Dinner. In the alumni *Record* and later the campus newspaper, the *Hilltop*, women students regularly noted their peers' "desire to cooperate and see this structure of womanhood grow."[20] As a result, within three short years the dinner became, in the eyes of Howard women, "the most important woman's function on the campus." A press release making this assertion proudly conveyed the evening's combination of frivolity and camaraderie:

> Women students, 300 strong, led by the marshal, marched into the Dining Hall singing college songs and giving lusty cheers for good old Howard. The women faculty and alumnae at places of honor in the Dining Hall applauded the marching students to the echo as they entered.
>
> The Program Committee arranged a most unique series of stunts by the various classes. The prize stunt was pulled off by the sophomore orchestra under the able direction of Ellen Hill. Miss Hill's baton, a brand new broom with a big red bow, waved gracefully over her players whose instruments of combs, tin pans, and bicycle pumps made music, "loud and clear."[21]

Such creative self-expression served a community-building function for the women in attendance, and alumnae were "greatly impressed" and supportive of the students.[22]

Inspiration was another key dimension of the dinners. Pathbreaking New Negro Women were invited to be guests of honor and embodied a sense of the possible for Howard women. These speakers included alumnae as well as other visionary leaders. Charlotte Hawkins Brown, the founder and principal of the Palmer Memorial Institute, a liberal arts day and boarding school in Sedalia, North Carolina, addressed the eighth Women's Dinner in 1929. At the thirteenth dinner in 1934 Clara Burrill Bruce, attorney and manager of the Paul Laurence Dunbar Apartments in Harlem (home to such major Black figures as W. E. B. Du Bois, A. Philip Randolph, and Matthew Henson), encouraged Howard women to pursue careers in law, business, and housing administration. During her student years at Boston University, Bruce had become the first African American woman president of the university's law review. Frances Grant, an instructor of English at Bordentown Industrial School in New Jersey and the first African American woman admitted to Phi Beta Kappa, spoke at the fourteenth dinner, in 1935. The operatic soprano Anne Wiggins Brown of *Porgy & Bess* fame, like Slowe a daughter of Baltimore, sang at the fifteenth dinner, in 1936, the last of Slowe's tenure.[23]

During the years the dinner was held, Howard women demonstrated important commitments to the event and each other. Articles about the dinner in the *Hilltop* described telegrams and letters sent by alumnae who "didn't forget to remember" the event.[24] By its seventh year, in November 1928, undergraduates were competing for a cup awarded to the class with the highest rate of attendance.[25] In 1929 the senior class made an impressive show of solidarity with three-quarters of its members present.[26] In a campus newspaper article, the reporter also highlighted the reactions of first-year women attendees of the ninth dinner as "rang[ing] from anticipation to the zenith of pleasure" and described juniors as "bubbling over with spirit and joy."[27] Reflecting their proud ownership of the event in its second decade, students announced the twelfth dinner in 1933 with a noontime parade through campus. At the dinner itself the students felt so comfortable in the atmosphere of intergenerational sisterly play that they made Dean Slowe and her assistant, Joanna Houston, "butts of [a] joke" about their fashion choices.[28] The recognition, rejoicing, and solidarity evident during the Women's Dinner stood in contrast to respectability's attempt to normalize struggle, isolation, and compliance. Embodying New Negro Woman sensibilities rendered the New Howard Woman an insistently modern figure.[29]

Defending an Original Design

As the dinner became a well-established and well-received tradition among Howard women, some men balked publicly at the gender exclusivity of the event. In the dinner's first year the *Record* reprinted a letter addressed to "My Doubly Dear Ladies," in which the writer adopted a sneeringly chivalrous tone to register his pronounced disapproval of the gathering: "This is the first time that I recall receiving a forewarning that men are forbidden even the thought of attending an exclusive feminine festal function.

We may be led to expect many strange things when the 'spare rib' sex announces its declaration of independence." Although the letter writer had already decided to forgo the dinner, he predicted with certainty that "the occasion will furnish ample opportunity for laughter on the part of the gods." He also insinuated that the only "wonder" of the evening would be the fashion worn by the women, writing, "Nay, nay, my dear ladies, in your dear costumes, this is not the wonder of the twentieth century. It is but the age old propensity of the one feminine to lure and beguile simple minded masculinity by the display of vanity and pride. It is as old as Eve and the red apple." His strong critique of the women's efforts and his own unyielding embrace of status quo gender relations trivialized the women's pleasure, labors, and intent. Moreover, he placed their actions in a framework of biblical patriarchy with its view of women, from Eve onward, as deceitful to their core. Dismissing what he mockingly termed an "Adamless dinner," this aggrieved man both understood and rejected the event as a challenge to the campus's patriarchal culture.[30]

Letters from other excluded men expressed much more support for the event. One addressed his "Dear Friends," and described the opportunity to observe the event from the balcony as a "kind invitation." For him the idea of "a Greater Howard" was not threatening, and he praised the organizers for their efforts: "As usual the women took the lead. It is my most sincere hope that the men will follow." A second man addressed his letter to Slowe directly and commented explicitly and approvingly on the invitation's "touch that gives your communication a laugh, a lilt, and a genuine touch of the human." He wished her "every success in this new and very promising movement" and, although unable to attend in person, stated that he would "be there in spirit." A third man described the event as "the beginning of a new day."[31]

Despite such evidence of support for the inaugural dinner, at several points during Slowe's tenure women students found the need to respond to criticism from Howard men. A student reporter for the *Hilltop's* 1930 Women's Edition, in an article under the headline "If Women May Speak," challenged the men's claims that the dinner was an unfairly exclusive event: "This has been labeled as undemocratic by some enterprising young men, yet cannot the women enjoy themselves with no men present, as the latter often do without the women, without being branded as undemocratic?" The decision to keep the dinner a women-only event was a shared and active commitment. As the reporter revealed, when a suggestion emerged to allow men to attend, "the women rallied to oppose it. At last they were doing something on their own." With pride this young journalist concluded that these actions demonstrated that Howard women had finally "attained a definite place right in the foreground of college activities."[32] This was both an exciting and powerful sign of their advancement on campus.

In the next academic year, a woman columnist challenged the demeaning characterization of the event by some men as "a frivolous affair" because it was not open to them. Reminding the men of the option to observe the event from the balcony, she invited such critics to actually "drop in on it for a minute and try to realize the breadth of its influence on the women and their sisters in the Big World."[33] In a November 1932 *Hilltop* article, a woman reporter proudly claimed that attendees engaging in "lusty songs . . . frightened the men away."[34] As the dinner entered its second decade, women students held to the belief that it served an essential purpose in its original, women-only design. As a synergistic link between current students and alumnae, it connected the space of undergraduate preparation with postgraduate possibilities.

Attended by more than four hundred women, the 1931 dinner marked a milestone in Slowe's efforts to transform campus culture and partner with Howard women. Students gave her a platinum brooch "in the design of a friendship circle." The setting included ten diamonds representing her decade of work. Because it allowed for the incorporation of additional gems for each subsequent year of service, the pin symbolized the shared vision between Slowe and the college women. The gift also recognized Slowe's major accomplishment of the 1931–32 academic year—the opening of three women's dorms that comprised the Women's Campus.[35] These newly erected buildings, alumna Margaret Jean Grooms later recalled, were "a memorial to [Slowe's] faith in Negro Womanhood" and aligned Howard women's residential environment with that of other "first class institutions."[36] In a departure from established tradition, the attendees at the 1931 dinner included "invited male guests."[37]

The last dinner over which Slowe would preside, in November 1936, attracted almost five hundred women and was the second largest in the event's history.[38] In addition to this strong attendance, Slowe received the fifteenth diamond for the friendship circle pin, as well as a gold watch.[39]

Alumnae sent telegrams expressing their regrets at being unable to attend, as well as checks to defray costs for current students.[40] Another particularly poignant indication of the event's significance for Howard women was a note from an 1871 alumna whose "health prohibited her attendance."[41] Although she had not been a student at Howard during Slowe's tenure, this woman regarded the dinner as a generative tradition she wanted to support. Evidently, the ideal of the New Howard Woman resonated with her too.

A Space of Their Own
The Women's Campus

Although the Women's Dinner was a visible and dramatic celebration of the New Howard Woman, realizing Slowe's philosophy of living more abundantly required many more shifts to the institution and its structures. During her inaugural year, Slowe worked with students to establish the Women's League, an inclusive association of women students. The league lobbied for women's collective interests and oversaw their extracurricular programming. As "the clearing house for all women's activities, and the agency for keeping alive traditional events of interest primarily to women," the league soon became the official sponsor of the Women's Dinner.[42] This body also organized three other annual extracurricular activities intended for the participation of all women students—the Christmas Vesper Service, the Women's Loan Fund, and the weeklong May Festival—as well as "smaller group activities, such as book reviews, teas, current events, coffee hours, lectures and discussions by faculty and outstanding women and men in various fields."[43] Like other deans of women, Slowe took a developmental approach to the college years and instituted a mentor system for selected seniors and first-year students.[44] Slowe chose rising juniors "on the basis of character and personality," and her office provided a "brief but intensive" training for these mentors. The goal was to help "build Howard Women who will be an asset not only to themselves, not only to this great institution, but to the society into which they will go."[45] Hilda Davis ('25), who was a sophomore in Slowe's inaugural year, recalled Slowe's successes: "With Dean Slowe we saw so many customs changed that we spoke among ourselves of our dean, not as Dean Slowe but as Dean Swift," as she put into practice her "pioneering . . . interest . . . in women's education and ideals."[46]

**Photo of 1936 May Festival queen,
Lauretta Wallace ('36).**
Courtesy of Scurlock Studio Records, Archives
Center, National Museum of American
History, Smithsonian Institution.

Committed to supporting the extracurricular growth of young women, Slowe—like her white dean peers—pressed for the establishment of a women's campus. In her first annual report in June 1923, she began lobbying the Howard University president to invest in dormitories that would not only provide adequate housing for women students but function as living-learning environments under their control.[47] She was concerned that the predominant social activities for Howard women consisted of dances sponsored by the men students and movies, and that more than three-quarters of the women students lived off campus, in part because of the lack of sufficient dormitory space.[48]

By spring 1931, Congress had appropriated enough money for Howard to build three new dorms for women.[49] For Slowe, their construction realized a "long planned dream," which a local newspaper described as closely aligned with Howard's institutional mission of "prepar[ing] leaders of the

colored race for a life devoid of prejudice and rich in culture and opportunities."[50] The establishment of the Women's Campus furthered a goal Slowe had long championed: attention to the needs and insights of Black women, which she contended was imperative to making progress in the condition of Black people.

With great anticipation, the Women's Campus opened at the start of the 1931–32 year. The three Georgian buildings provided housing for three hundred women students. Amenities included a coffee shop, dining room, infirmary, beauty salon, and laundry facilities; reception, guest, and assembly space; and elevator access to the upper floors. Students' rooms were equipped with hot running water and closets.[51] Although the dorms provided the conveniences of modern living, more important to Slowe was that these new buildings operated as "a laboratory for practical education in human relationships."[52] Management of these living-learning spaces fell to the Students' House Government Association. This practice was in line with the deans of women's focus on young women's self-governance, rather than institutional surveillance of them, and the development of students' self-direction, rather than their subjection to adult control. In consultation with the college-educated women dorm directors on Slowe's staff, the House Government Association determined standards of behavior.[53] Although Slowe believed rules were important for maintaining "the common good," she refused to allow them to operate as concessions to "the immoderate conservatism of men in administration."[54] Slowe believed students should have ways to "become an active and useful part of the University" from their first weeks on campus.[55] The dean maintained that Black women needed opportunities to develop "a solidarity and an independence . . . through purposeful activities," rather than through infantilizing rules and regulations.[56]

Creating Spaces for Recreation and Play

Along with her white peers, Slowe encouraged physical activity and play as important means of developing college women's "powers of initiative and self-direction."[57] The end of her first decade in office saw the establishment in 1931 of the Women's Athletic League, whose motto was "A Game for Every Girl, and Every Girl in a Game."[58] Intramural sports included archery, swimming, basketball, tennis, and field hockey.[59] Other campus leisure opportunities combined gender pride and leadership with fun. The Women's League organized the Gay Nineties ball, for which Howard women dressed in the "bustles and laces" of their grandmothers' generation, as well as a costume ball open to all students.[60] A memorable 1936 Valentine's Day party challenged gender norms as attendees invited their own escorts, and it drew supportive attention in the *Hilltop*: "The girls did all of the requesting [of dance partners]. At first they were a little shy (?), but by the time that the tin horns and confetti were distributed, everyone had caught the spirit of the party."[61] Howard women also took their play to open campus spaces. In May 1930 graduating senior women donned costumes for Frivolity Day, which included ringing bells and "playing childhood games." Although "few of the boys dressed," their lack of participation did not seem to dampen the fun the women had.[62]

Dean Slowe created even more opportunities to further institutionalize a "feminine atmosphere in the college." In her first three years she reached

Howard University Women's Hockey Squad, ca. 1930.
Photo by the Scurlock Studio, courtesy of the Moorland-Spingarn Research Center,
Howard University Archives, Howard University, Washington, D.C.

out to the few women faculty, as well as the wives of Howard professors, and organized the Woman's Cooperative Council. Meeting monthly, this group hosted socials for women students.[63] Regularizing interactions between the college students and these adult women was part of Slowe's goal to support young women's development as individuals and members of a robust community.

Archival evidence suggests that adult women welcomed much playfulness among Howard undergraduates. In February 1932 college women presented a Talent Night program consisting of skits, original poetry, dance and music routines, dramatic readings, and acrobatic feats. A *Hilltop* article described the event as "a wonderful exhibition of co-operation both among the girls and with the faculty."[64] In fall 1934, the Women's Faculty Club organized a party for the college women. The program included a Chinese gong, peanuts tossed to be caught, "shouts and cries," games, stunts, eating contests, a competition to construct clothing out of newspaper, and making drawings while blindfolded.[65] These collaborative gatherings reflected adult Black women's investment in the potential of young women, to whom one Women's Dinner speaker referred as the "flower of womanhood of a struggling race."[66] Conveying a similar faith in her peers, one student asserted, "The chances for Negro women, the hope of future generations, rests with the younger women."[67] These activities normalized voiceful fun and gender solidarity in contrast to the atmosphere that emerged in campus sororities.

Beyond a Sororal Womanhood
The Women's League

Howard University holds the distinction of being home to three Black sororities—Alpha Kappa Alpha (founded in 1908), Delta Sigma Theta (1913), and Zeta Phi Beta (1920). Part of what accounts for the dinner's success from its inception was that some students were already exhibiting the qualities of the New Negro Woman. In fall 1922, the same semester as the inaugural dinner, Delta Sigma Theta acquired a new residence. In her account of the significance of the space to the college women, a student writer for the alumni magazine pointed to important shifts in the self-concepts of contemporary young Black women: "The women of today have a broader field into which to enter than had the women of a few decades ago. Their duties are not restricted to the maintaining of the home life. The women of today play a vital part in the affairs of the world. Much is expected of them." For this soror, service extended well beyond the domestic sphere. Such breadth of engagement was "the price the world asks in return for the advantages offered."[68]

Valuing and seeking to make social contributions outside the home or the Black community was not a new conviction for the sorority. Founded on January 13, 1913, the sorority's first public act was to participate in the Woman Suffrage Procession in Washington, D.C., less than two months later. Accompanied by their adviser, the activist Mary Church Terrell, twenty-two founding members joined the parade among their white peers, rather than at the back of the procession. In defiance of parade organizers' attempts to placate segregationists, the sorority women marched under their own banner. As soror Florence Letcher Toms recalled, "We marched that day in order that women might come into their own, because we believed that women not only needed an education, but they needed a broader horizon in which they may use that education. And the right to vote would give them that privilege."[69] As Toms asserted, the sorors' participation declared not only their existence but their expectations of inclusion and equality within movements they viewed as aligned with their own sense of possibility.[70] A lesser status was unacceptable to them.

Even with Delta Sigma Theta's embrace of a Black woman–centered spirit of growth and ambition, as well as Slowe's own undergraduate contributions to Alpha Kappa Alpha, the dean sought a wider institutional basis for her New Howard Woman ideal. Unlike sororities with membership criteria and exclusions, the Women's Dinner was intentionally open to all Howard women, and it cultivated an inclusive definition of scholastic womanhood through new traditions. Irrespective of individual women's campus group affiliations, the dinner "emphasiz[ed] the spirit of sisterhood among Howard women."[71] Slowe believed it essential that Howard women invest in a visible and far-ranging gender solidarity. The dean's work focused on "building up a woman's consciousness in the University."[72]

An April 1937 *Hilltop* editorial laid bare a men-centeredness that weakened collective action within sororities. As a result, according to the writer, too many of these women's groups were being "used as servants, in fact, as 'stooges' for fraternities to further the leadership of males." The editorialist reminded her audience that at their founding, "sororities were organized for service to the community, not as congregations of cliques inviting members [to be] judged on the basis of being good looking, and amenable to control."[73] These regressive elements in the campus's gender culture made it necessary for Howard women to create alternatives to it. For Slowe, activities that fostered expressiveness as well as community among women were critical for them to live more abundantly. Through a "common bond of sympathy and fellowship," all students, faculty, and alumnae could take on the individual ambition and collective consciousness of being New Howard Women.[74]

The National Association of College Women
Advocating for an Educated
New Negro Womanhood at HBCUs

As a New Negro Woman and the first African American dean of women in the United States, Slowe led the incorporation of this position at other HBCUs. In April 1923 she approached the College Alumnae Club (CAC) of

Dean Slowe with members of the National Association of Women's Deans and Advisers of Colored Schools, Wilberforce University, March 1936.
Courtesy of the Moorland-Spingarn Research Center, Howard University Archives, Howard University, Washington, D.C.

Washington, D.C., and convinced the regional organization to establish a new federation, the National Association of College Women (NACW). The central focus of the NACW was to advocate specifically for the educational interests, needs, and advancement of Black women students, faculty, and administrators. From 1924 to 1929, Slowe served as president of the NACW, and she remained an executive committee member for the whole of her career.

Although modeling itself on the American Association of University Women (AAUW) and using similar membership criteria, including graduation from a recognized liberal arts institution, the NACW emphasized the specific needs and aspirations of New Negro Women. Upholding Black women's capacity for leadership, Slowe outlined three major priorities for the nascent NACW: the recruitment of "deserving and capable" young Black women and raising money to help them attend college; equity for women students and faculty on campuses; and fostering interracial understanding with white college alumnae. To promote such Black women–centered gender solidarity, Slowe encouraged NACW members to "face the future boldly."[75] She and other founding members of the association saw college-educated women as "constructive workers, not blind followers."[76]

During Slowe's career the NACW organized annual spring meetings at HBCUs and published a journal of its proceedings. Advocating for social leadership rather than conventional racial uplift, the New Negro Women members of the NACW promoted the "self-determination, respect, and advancement of college-trained African-American women."[77] Making good on its core charge to elevate the standing of Black college women, the NACW became the parent organization to two major initiatives: surveying women's experiences as students, faculty, and administrators at HBCUs, and the 1929 founding of the National Association of Women's Deans and Advisors of Colored Schools (NAWDACS).[78] Meeting annually until 1954, the NAWDACS promoted the work of women deans within Black secondary schools and HBCUs.[79]

Refusing Nineteenth-Century Gender Logics
The New Negro Woman's Vision
of Higher Education for Black Women

Despite the support she received from students and alumnae, Slowe's philosophy of living more abundantly was a striking departure from the much more deferential posture that Black communities and higher education institutions expected from African American women. In a series that began with an invited lecture on race and education at Teachers College in 1931, and subsequently included two papers published in 1933 and 1937, Slowe expressed most clearly her critique of the status of Black women's education and the importance of deans' efforts at HBCUs. In these works Slowe drew attention to a series of outdated yet common beliefs about Black women that were evident in their communities of origin as well as in the colleges and universities they attended.

Like deans of women across the country, Slowe insisted that college women deserved leadership opportunities and the preparation to pursue new professions as graduates. However, the case for Black women at HBCUs was unique: Founded in the decades following the Civil War to produce graduates who would operate within the confines of a racially segregated society, these institutions—Slowe contended—urgently needed to update their work to address the conditions and problems of "the modern world," the twentieth century.[80] With regard to women students in particular, Slowe asserted that HBCUs had yet to recognize the social influence of industrialization and suffrage and as a result failed to "prepare Negro college women for intelligent participation and leadership" in a society in which they worked and legally had the right to vote.[81]

Slowe raised concerns about the gender ideologies that HBCUs promoted and resisted questioning. These institutions needed to accept, "whether they like it or not, the life that women are leading today is different from that which was led by their grandmothers." Operating with antiquated nineteenth-century gender logics, HBCUs reinforced cultural attitudes that Slowe found troubling and deeply out of step with societal trends and needs. In contrast she believed such Black-serving institutions needed to equip their women students to "be ready to make their contribution not only to the home but also to the economic, political, and civic life of their communities."[82]

Slowe also maintained that Black college women had a "peculiar experience" in terms of their history and socialization that required they have access to leadership opportunities. Traditional gender attitudes prevailed in Black women's home communities, such that "many parents still believe that the definition of woman found in an eighteenth century dictionary is true today: 'Woman, the female of man. See man.'" Furthermore, Slowe faulted obsolete gender views and conservative religious philosophies for "suppressing . . . [Black women's] own powers." Taken together, these conditions among Black women matriculants normalized an approach to life that Slowe criticized as "the psychology of inaction rather than that of active curiosity."[83]

Such antiquated views of Black womanhood in students' home communities were met with equally concerning attitudes at the coeducational HBCUs a majority of them attended. Patriarchal outlooks on modernity and gender greatly shaped—and in most cases hampered—the ability of women matriculants to realize their contributions as individuals in a changing society. Slowe believed in Black women's leadership potential, and she expected colleges to cultivate this capacity. NACW survey responses, however, revealed a deeply paternalistic neglect of women's needs at HBCUs. The survey found that only 41 percent of reporting institutions offered specific opportunities for women to engage in self-governance, a pillar of the deans of women movement. From that statistic Slowe concluded that too few schools were providing Black women with extracurricular outlets for "exercising initiative, independence, and self-direction while in college." These reactionary attitudes and trends resulted in HBCUs' failing to "train [women] to understand the world as it now is, and to aid it in changing for the better." Because she believed Black women should exercise choice in their social contributions, Slowe rejected cultural constructions of them as "adjuncts of 'man'" on the grounds that "modern life forces them to be individuals in much the same sense as men are individuals."[84] Her notion of "social usefulness" took form in many domains, the home as well as the new professions and the world of business.[85]

For Slowe, a modern college education needed not only to support career preparation but to promote self-direction, which required that Black women students exercise initiative and independence in their decision making.[86] As a result, she balked at the preponderance of meddlesome rules imposed on women at HBCUs. "Designed to control their conduct," these regulations withheld "that necessary opportunity for making independent choices without which real freedom of action cannot be developed. When a college woman cannot be trusted to go shopping without a chaperone she is not likely to develop powers of leadership."[87] Slowe believed it was the obligation of colleges and universities to prepare Black women for whatever "sphere of life they will occupy after graduation."[88] In not specifying a particular kind of career trajectory, she revealed her fundamental belief that Black women alone should determine the environment—whether a home, community, or workplace—to which they would contribute their skills. To this end Slowe urged Howard women to develop independence of judgment and to exert the "effort . . . to be an individual and not merely a woman following the man."[89]

To illustrate the anachronistic nineteenth-century thinking of twentieth-century Black communities and schools, Slowe cited what were likely the comments of Howard's first African American president, Mordecai Wyatt Johnson.[90] Throughout her tenure Johnson stood in opposition to her expansion of the educational and vocational opportunities available to Black college women. The unnamed administrator referenced in Slowe's 1931 talk asserted that because women should "be trained to be good wives and mothers," they did not require exposure to the "male subjects" of the social sciences.[91] For Slowe, such attitudes pressed Black women into "curricular corset[s]" and were a consequence of women's attending schools "almost exclusively administered by men," who themselves were unwilling to recognize "the changed status of women in the modern world."[92] Rather than advocate for a rejection of the classical liberal arts focus on the humanities and sciences, Slowe argued for the inclusion of political science, economics, and sociology, as well as rural studies, to develop understanding of the world and the tools to take informed action in it.[93]

Slowe recognized that racial respectability shaped both Black women's codes of behavior and their professional aspirations. She criticized the way Black women's education was diverted from subject areas more widely accepted for whites and Black men, largely based on ongoing discriminatory attitudes, rather than Black women's interest, innate ability, or potential. Because they "labored under the double handicap of race and sex—a Negro in a white world and a female in a male world," college-educated Black women tended to be pragmatic in their career pursuits, and in many communities teaching in segregated public schools exemplified a respectable job.[94] To disrupt this pattern, Slowe's office provided Howard women with vocational counseling and exposure to other occupations.[95] In her commitment to fostering Black women's discernment of their "life's work," Slowe encouraged their consideration of careers such as accounting, dentistry, journalism, law, medicine, and writing.[96] She also used the Women's Dinner strategically to recognize guest speakers who embodied Black women's accomplishments in a range of fields.

In 1930 Howard held a one-day Women's Vocational Conference, which featured representatives from fields such as public health nursing, research, and medicine, and their talks focused explicitly on "the education of women for the modern world."[97] A *Hilltop* article noted that the event attended especially to first-year women students "with the hope that they will select their life's work with more intelligence and vision."[98] Hilda Davis, a Howard alumna and future dean of women at Shaw University (1932–36) and Talladega College (1936–52), recalled the impact of these vocational visits by "women outstanding in various fields": the guests spent several days on campus and "enter[ed] into the lives of the students in a way that would not have been possible by a casual visit."[99] Slowe supplemented such guest presentations with annual interviews of each student "to see whether or not what she has chosen will lead her where she wishes to go." In a memo outlining her duties, Slowe acknowledged that such personalized outreach "consumes a great deal of time" but concluded that it was "very much worth while."[100] In these ways Slowe sought to build on Black women's sense of social responsibility but extend it beyond teaching. She maintained a commitment to a much wider sphere of purposeful, remunerative work and acted upon her deep reservations about the limitation of vocational options for Black college women. In attending to her

Dean Slowe with members of the Dean of Women's Club, 1930.
Courtesy of the Moorland-Spingarn Research Center, Howard University Archives,
Howard University, Washington, D.C.

students' specific talents, Slowe affirmed their desires for achievement and emphasized the personal joy and social benefit of pursuing their purpose.

In spring 1930 Slowe took the initiative to create a professional pipeline into deaning by offering an undergraduate course at Howard University. The inaugural group of enrolled women consisted of eleven undergraduates and Johanna Houston, a 1924 alumna who from 1928 to 1936 served as Slowe's assistant dean of women.[101] Although Teachers College, the leading institution offering coursework in deaning, matriculated Black women, Slowe saw a particular need for cultivating young southern Black women's interest in the profession. Her hope was that Howard would become a "model department for the training of deans of women" in HBCUs.[102]

Despite her many efforts to expand the vocational trajectories for Howard women, Slowe found that the overwhelming majority pursued traditional paths, much like their peers at other HBCUs. A 1931 address that drew specifically on Howard women students' courses of study and intended careers revealed that of 153 first-years, 142 were pursuing teaching largely because "it is the only occupation which is open to them with few handicaps."[103] Data from the spring 1937 semester quantified women's enrollment in the social sciences from a low of 3 percent in economics to a high of 28 percent in psychology. Although these numbers surpassed the averages Slowe reported in a 1933 paper aggregating data across HBCUs, Slowe found them reflective not simply of societal racism in the workplace, which resulted in most graduates' "crowd[ing] into the teaching profession," but of what she termed "defects in the Negro college," which included a failure to expose women to new fields outside teaching and social work.[104] However, rather than resign herself to the stratification of the labor market and conventional cultural expectations about women's work, Slowe persisted in offering vocational guidance and exposure to help Black women navigate new and developing career opportunities.

Conclusion

Recognition, visibility, and voice were key themes in Slowe's work on campus and in higher education as an unapologetic advocate for educated Black womanhood. An unassailable belief in Black women's worth guided her efforts in creating new traditions and geographies defined by Black women's possibility rather than the socially circulating claims of their deficiency or inadequacy. Students appreciated Slowe's extracurricular investment in their development because, as one alumna recalled, the dean interacted with them as a coworker rather than a superior. Given that Slowe had adopted a developmental stance toward the young women, they "could talk sympathetically with her as I did with my pals."[105] Slowe did not endorse a college life unduly focused on coeducational parties and dances, a point of contention for some Howard women.[106] However, she did have—as Hilda Davis recalled—"the courage to allow young people freedom, yes freedom even to make some mistakes. We soon learned that, though she might let us stumble in our attempts to solve problems for ourselves, she was ever beside us to catch us before we fell."[107] In her forms of student outreach, Slowe labored against a cultural inertia and exhorted Black women to "take a place as individuals in this institution, and to prepare themselves for their debut to the world after college."[108] She expected them, as New

Howard Women, to determine their unique strengths and capacities. To spur this individuality among Howard women, Slowe elected to "look up, laugh, and love, and lift."[109]

The impact of living more abundantly, recalled one alumna, was that Dean Slowe "got us really interested in being women and demanding our rights as women. . . . You know everything was very male-tailored until Lucy Slowe came."[110] Rather than remain silent and accommodate herself to a racialized and gendered structure of inequality, the New Howard Woman—in the person of Dean Slowe and her women graduates—took up the charge that Black women were not anyone's subordinate but "levelly human."[111] This ideal resonated with most Howard women, who worked with Slowe to establish the New Howard Woman's presence on campus. Slowe's vision of educated Black womanhood rejected many dominant expectations of what Black women should be, think, and do in the company of both whites and Black men. A leader and agent in her own right, the New Howard Woman embodied a twentieth-century willingness to lean into her self-actualization and social usefulness. As the next two chapters examine, the dean's unflinching commitment to Black women's self-determination challenged many of higher education's entrenched racialized and gendered beliefs about human worth.

CHAPTER 3

RACE WORK IS WOMEN'S WORK
DEANING AND THE COLOR LINE

And she could draw a circle which took others in even
though some might try to draw one with her out.
—Kathryn G. Heath to Marion T. Wright, September 6, 1962

For the problem of the Twentieth Century is the problem of the color-line.
—W. E. B. Du Bois, *The Souls of Black Folk*

Among Slowe's papers is a professional photograph measuring eleven by
nineteen inches. Taken by the Black-owned and -operated Scurlock Pho-
tographic Studio (1911–94) in Washington, D.C., the image documents an
important moment in Slowe's career—her February 1932 welcome of sixty
deans of women who had traveled to Washington, D.C., for the sixteenth
annual convention of their professional organization, the National Association of Deans of Women (NADW).[1] While in town, the deans visited the
Howard campus, where the focus of their tour was the Women's Campus,
the three new women's dorms that had opened in the fall term of that academic year. With the establishment of a geography specifically for Howard women students' lives outside the classroom, Slowe had achieved a
major milestone in her work of transforming the university to meet wom-
en's needs.

The interracial gathering captured by the photo might even be considered racially traitorous, given that the deans had assembled to mark a Black
woman's accomplishment.[2] A further indication of an encouraging—and
for its time a striking—example of women engaging as equals across the

DELEGATES OF 16TH ANNIVERSARY SESSION
OF NATIONAL ASSOCIATION OF DEANS
OF WOMEN VISIT HOWARD UNIVERSITY FEB 18 1932
SCURLOCK. PHOTO.

**Deans belonging to the National Association of Deans of Women visit
the Women's Campus, Howard University, February 18, 1932.**
Photo by the Scurlock Studio, courtesy of the Moorland-Spingarn Research Center,
Howard University Archives, Howard University, Washington, D.C.

early twentieth-century color line is that Slowe is standing proudly left
of center, with the prominent white dean, Thyrsa Wealtheow Amos, of
the University of Pittsburgh, next to her. A highly regarded leader in the
dean of women movement, Amos was also an instructor in the Teachers
College summer program Slowe had attended. During Slowe's tenure,
she and Amos remained in contact and made several visits to each other's
campus. When Slowe wrote to Amos in June 1931 about breaking ground
for the dormitories, Amos expressed her desire to "have any part in their
dedication."[3]

Although there is archival evidence of collegiality between Slowe and her
white peers, the NADW—like other early twentieth-century New Women
organizations in the work of social reform—operated from a stance of white
racial superiority. As a result, such moments of New Negro Women and

New Women engaging in partnership were elusive and not representative of Slowe's ongoing interactions with the NADW and its members. Rather, throughout the whole of her fifteen-year career, Slowe confronted tacit, and at times overt, racial arrogance among New Women deans.

The Color Line Runs through Us
In Search of Interracial Gender Solidarity

In her charge to the National Association of College Women (NACW), which she had founded in the spring of her first year as dean, Slowe exhorted its members to pursue three initiatives—to encourage college attendance among young Black women; to institutionalize gender fairness in higher education, largely through the appointment of deans of women at all colleges and universities; and to work actively toward interracial understanding. She believed college-educated women in particular were well positioned to promote "peace and harmony among the races in the United States."[4] In these hopes Slowe was not blindly optimistic or ignorant of the realities of racism. However, she understood the maintenance of the color line as a learned behavior that operated in violation of the tenets of a multiracial, pluralistic democracy. And as an educator Slowe believed in the possibility of social change through informed, honest interactions between race and gender groups.

The regenerative potential of higher education was the focus of Slowe's remarks at the first NADW meeting she attended as dean in February 1923. As the *Howard University Record* summarized with great pride, during a panel addressing the subject of foreign students, Slowe emphasized "the right of every student to be judged by his individual worth [rather] than by his racial affiliations." To the general New Woman principle articulated by her NADW peers, that higher education should encourage personal development, Slowe added that "every university . . . should be a cosmopolitan center" encouraging mutuality "based on knowledge and not upon prejudice."[5] Although she understood that the color line coursed through all American institutions, Slowe saw colleges and universities as unique venues for change, where knowledge and actual interaction could supplant myths and distortions. As a result, racial segregation had no place in her conceptualization of higher education in the twentieth century.

At the same session on foreign students, Anne Dudley Blitz, then dean of women at the University of Kansas, gave a paper in which she described how the Women's Student Government Association of her campus had solicited her support "for segregating the negro students in the classroom, laboratory, and library." Expressing dismay at this request, Blitz cautioned that "where the students have partial or full control, segregation shows its head more and more insistently."[6]

Although she was voicing criticism of the women students for their racial exclusivity, Blitz subsequently revealed her own troubling anti-Black beliefs. She portrayed African Americans as culturally bereft, believing that they had lost any African traditions and developed forms of music and folklore that were "more a negro perversion of an American product" than a genuinely unique contribution. In her disparagement of Black people, Blitz failed to acknowledge the realities of slavery and segregation. She also conveyed racist concerns about intermarriage, specifically between white women and Black men. She asserted that such women tended to be of "a lower type of white" and predicted that the children of these unions would face exile from both groups.[7] Significantly, her focus completely eclipsed any attention to white men's long terroristic history of perpetrating sexualized violence against Black women or to Black women students' existence on her campus.

Twelve years later Slowe and Blitz would exchange letters about the housing of Black undergraduate women at the University of Minnesota, where Blitz served as dean of women from 1923 to 1949. In October 1936 Slowe appealed to Blitz on behalf of "the daughter of a very dear friend of mine," carefully describing the young woman in respectable terms—she was "financially able to live in the dormitory and [came from] a family that has a very fine background."[8] However, Blitz—described in a retrospective institutional history as having a "striking . . . zeal for segregation"— refused to accommodate Slowe's request.[9] Although Blitz was invoking the Minnesota regents' policy-setting authority against integrated housing, she also evinced a telling lack of investment in Black women students' actual needs and realities. Rather, she focused on securing off-campus housing for these students and reported to Slowe: "I found a pleasant room where Elizabeth and another colored girl could room near the campus, but for some reason or other they did not take it, and they are living, I believe, over at the Phyllis Wheatley House, the center for our colored population."[10] In her letter Blitz exhibited little curiosity about or real knowledge of the young Black women's situation: she displayed no interest in knowing why they rejected her alternative to campus housing, their exact place of residence, or the reasons they elected instead to board in the Black community.

In her November 1936 response, Slowe both highlighted and took issue with the flawed and hypocritical educational policy to which Blitz appealed in her avoidance of responsibility. Given that the university was in the North—"a sector of the United States which is not cursed with the tradition of racial prejudice"—Slowe had expected it to be "very broadminded." Finding that the North operated with the same racial logics of the South, she expressed her outrage: "It seems to me that a university is failing in a fundamental duty when it adopts a policy which perpetuates racial intolerance. You realize, of course, that I am not blaming you for this policy for I am mindful of the fact that we Deans of Women are subject to our Boards of Trustees, but I certainly regret that you are placed in the position which I believe is contrary to your own feeling in the matter."[11] Slowe made clear her personal rejection of segregation and insinuated that Blitz felt—or should feel—similarly aggrieved about the unfairness of the housing policy. Segregation was, Slowe insisted to her peer, wholly incompatible with their charge as educators.

Despite the absence of a response from Blitz, other materials suggest the white dean's personal investment in residential segregation. After she similarly was denied campus housing by Blitz, Charlotte Crump—another African American woman student and the daughter of a St. Paul, Minnesota, physician—published a thinly fictionalized account of her experiences in the university's *Literary Review*. Subsequently reprinted in the National Urban League's *Opportunity* magazine, "This Free North" lamented Crump's initial faith in northern whites: "Why did I think that white college students would be different from other white people? Why did I naively believe they would be more tolerant here? Could I have thought that a university such as this—with the opportunity it gives for breadth of social outlook—would offer that barely glimpsed utopia of minority groups, a place prejudice-free?"[12]

Crump pointed out that while no official policy barred Black students from residing on campus, administrators claimed that white students objected to interracial housing. She also mentioned encountering an unnamed woman, likely Blitz, whose false "sweetness" made a Black woman classmate who was denied housing "squirm." The lack of support Crump and other Black students received from the campus compelled them to create the Council of Negro Students to press for recognition of their unmet needs.[13]

Upon learning about the publication, Blitz took grievous offense at Crump's characterization of her experiences at the university and rebuked the student in a letter: "I wish that you would come in and talk to me about your story in the *Literary Review*. . . . There are some misstatements there that I feel sure you would not want to have, if you had taken the trouble to verify your facts."[14] As in her exchanges with Slowe, Blitz demonstrated an arrogant belief that her own outlook and actions were correct. Such a stance stood far afield from the interracial contact and mutual understanding that Slowe pressed her white peers to develop, yet it was quite normative within the NADW. Against such racist attitudes promoting Black women's social invisibility Slowe repeatedly insisted that her white colleagues commit to ending both race and gender prejudice as central tasks of the modern university and the profession of deaning.

As the first Black member of the NADW, Slowe attracted queries from her white peers regarding matters they perceived as uncomfortably racial. In November 1930 Lucy Jenkins Franklin, Boston University's dean of women, wrote to Slowe asking for guidance on what would constitute "proper housing" for Black women students. Franklin had solicited the preferences of the young women in question as well as the advice of local Black organizations. No clear course of action emerged: some advocated separate housing to protect the Black women from hostilities their white peers were likely to perpetrate, while others recommended including the young women in the standard housing plans. Franklin reached out to Slowe as one who could examine the issue "from the standpoint of an educator and one who considered the welfare and happiness of the girl herself."[15]

In her response Slowe referenced what she considered the "fundamental principle" of higher education—a focus on individuals, not races—which was itself a tool for gauging moral action at the college and university levels. She then advised that the Black women students be housed along with their white peers, insisting that "under no circumstances should the University suggest to the Negro student that it looks upon him in any other way than as a worthy individual who is an integral part of the University family. . . . [In higher education] there should be no taint of segregation on account of race." Although not unaware of the probability that the young women would face insensitive slights and even outright rejection from their white peers, Slowe squarely maintained that the university itself carried the obligation to intervene and create a hospitable learning-living environment for all students. In no uncertain terms she declared, "If the other girls of the University have these prejudices, it is the business of the University to rid them of these prejudices as a part of their liberal education."[16]

Slowe clarified to her NADW colleague that the responsibility to educate meant that colleges and universities needed to broaden their students beyond what she called the narrowness with which they entered. As a result, she baldly insisted to Dean Franklin that "to deny them [white students] the opportunity" of widening their social knowledge "would be tragic indeed." Slowe's closing lines further pushed Franklin to see herself not as a passive administrator but as a campus and social leader: "By so doing you would be demonstrating that Boston University is in truth a University and that it is interested in the highest development of its individual students."[17]

In encouraging Franklin to view campus belonging as a core right of students, Slowe challenged her colleague to realize that race was always a part of deans' work and that the exclusion of the Black women students was fundamentally in conflict with deans' professional commitment to supporting educational opportunity for women. Through such advocacy, Slowe asserted, Franklin would be "making a real contribution to friendly race relationships, which is one of our most pressing social problems at the present time."[18] Two years after this exchange, Hilda A. Davis, a 1925 Howard alumna and Slowe protégé, enrolled in Boston University's Alice Freeman Palmer Course for Deans of Women.[19] For an assignment she conducted a "survey of living conditions for Negro women students in white colleges and universities."[20] One wonders whether Slowe's correspondence with Franklin influenced both women's interest in the significance of campus housing for inclusive education. Notably, Franklin was also among the NADW members who toured the new women's dormitories at Howard University in 1932.[21]

Christian Sisterhood
Participatory Belonging and the YWCA

During her career as dean Slowe served on the national board of the Young Women's Christian Association (YWCA). In its demonstrated and pioneering structural commitments to fostering interracial cooperation among women, the YWCA, not the NADW, was the organization in which she experienced meaningful mutual regard and belonging among white women peers.

Introduced to the United States from England in 1858, the YWCA promoted a concept of Christian sisterhood that encompassed women's vocational opportunities, physical well-being, and community.[22] Initially, the YWCA focused on intraracial and cross-class outreach in its reform efforts. However, the prodding and persistence of Black women—who held their white peers to the organization's stated principles of "love for all and the oneness of all in Christ"—helped transform it by the mid-twentieth century into the largest and most inclusive "multiracial and interfaith women's organization" in the United States.[23] In this considerable shift from a segregated to an interracial organization, the YWCA came to embrace racial justice "as a central mission, rather than an awkward aside."[24]

With the first college chapter founded in 1873, the YWCA also made early inroads into women's higher education.[25] YWCA campus chapters, which predated the hiring of trained deans of women, connected students to an informal network of community women who offered housing and counsel. Upon the emergence of deaning as a profession in the early twentieth century, and given their common focus on women's empowerment, deans of women typically served as the adviser to the YWCA student groups on their campuses.[26]

College chapters of the YWCA were popular associations across both historically Black and white colleges and universities. In 1912 Black colleges had more than fifty YWCA student group chapters; after HBCUs added thirty more a year later, the organization reached more than half the enrolled population of Black women students.[27] By 1924 the YWCA had 681 domestic and international campus associations, with 105 housed at Black institutions of higher education.[28] Data from Slowe's own NACW-sponsored survey confirmed the YWCA's centrality to Black women's college careers at HBCUs. In 1930, whereas almost 70 percent of reporting institutions had a

YWCA chapter, just over a quarter had sororities, and only 7 percent supported a women's league.[29]

Although the evangelical grounding of the YWCA made it attractive to the conservatism of many colleges, its notion of Christian sisterhood could also affirm women's interracial solidarity. The National Student Council (NSC) led the college division of the YWCA, and as early as 1915 student chapters sponsored an interracial convention.[30] In May 1924, after the NSC's Commission on Standards completed a two-year study of the social interests of college women members, it determined that "many students are concerned and are eager to find the power to face certain great problems such as racial relations, marriage, war, [and] individual freedom versus group loyalty."[31] In promoting an interracial sisterhood, such student members stood against national and local practices that more often maintained a color line.[32]

At the start of her tenure at Howard, Slowe served on the board of the NSC as well as on the YWCA's National Council on Colored Work, which oversaw the operation of "colored associations," fostered interracial education, and linked chapters across the color line.[33] For twelve years, from 1925 to 1937, Slowe represented the NSC at the annual national conventions of the Committee on the Cause and Cure of War, a coalition of nine Progressive Era women's organizations.[34] The regularity of her attendance reflected not only her shared embrace of the ideal of peace promoted by the committee but also the specific and atypical belonging she experienced within the YWCA. After returning from the inaugural conference in 1925, Slowe described her experiences to Leslie Blanchard, the executive secretary of the NSC and a 1912 Stanford graduate whose own relationship with the YWCA began during her college years.[35]

With much enthusiasm Slowe conveyed to her white colleague how the YWCA was distinctive in its strides to incorporate Black women. Her comments highlighted her subjective sense of acceptance, which she found both heartening and noteworthy. Among other self-described "liberal minded" New Women organizations in attendance, Slowe wrote, the YWCA was "the only one that included in its delegates a representation of the colored race." Because the YWCA was "attempting to look at all races as one family," it was "making a real contribution to the solving of our national and international problems as they concerned misunderstandings between races."[36] Throughout her tenure at Howard, Slowe would reach out to

Blanchard. And in ways much more forthcoming than she would be with other white women deans, Slowe expressed her disappointments with the NADW's ongoing failures to extend full membership to her and the Black deans who followed in her professional footsteps.

Crossing the NADW's Color Line

Slowe's interracial vision for higher education and her connections to the YWCA—rather than the NADW, her primary professional organization—facilitated some of her most successful engagements with white college-educated women. In 1925 she addressed the Club of Prospective Deans at Teachers College to make "a plea . . . for better race relationships between colored and white women of this country." In her remarks Slowe presented her ideal of colleges as inclusive spaces where "students of all races would come together for the purpose of discovering that which is good in members of different racial groups." Racial exclusion was a policy she roundly condemned for violating higher education's "boasted principles of liberality and rationalism." In the study and resolution of racial problems, she asserted that college women and deans of women should "lead the way" and not pursue "the method of evasion, indifference and ignorance" evident in many white-dominated settings.[37]

Significantly, despite Slowe's membership in the NADW and her professional contacts with the faculty of Teachers College, her opportunity to address the club of prospective deans emerged from her ties to the YWCA, and in particular her relationship with Juliette Derricotte. A fellow African American and graduate of Teachers College, Derricotte was a national student secretary for the YWCA.[38] In this role from 1918 to 1929, she traveled to, and worked with, the student branches of the YWCA housed at both HBCUs and many white colleges.[39] Derricotte would go on to serve as dean of women at Fisk University from 1929 to 1931.

In her communication with Derricotte, Slowe expressed how she was "so much interested in the possibility of speaking to the group." Despite being "as poor as can be," she offered to cover the costs of her travel in order to give "our side of this race problem to such a representative group as would be found in Miss Sturtevant's class."[40] Sarah M. Sturtevant (1881–1942) was a professor of education at Teachers College and a member of NADW. For Slowe to address deans in training—alumnae preparing to direct undergraduate women's development—was to perhaps broaden their consciousness of, and commitment to, the realities of sexism and racism in higher education. In her appeal to these educators to improve interracial relations, Slowe was likely encouraged by the existence of white women like Blanchard whose social outlooks were shaped through their own undergraduate involvement with the YWCA.

During the spring of 1925 Slowe followed her Teachers College appeal to prospective deans with similar lectures to women students and faculty at the University of Delaware, University of Pittsburgh, and Women's College of Newark, New Jersey. The titles of these addresses—"The Responsibility of the College Woman in Race Relations," "The College Woman's Responsibility in Race Relations," and "The Responsibility of College Women in Race Relationships"—demonstrated Slowe's radical refusal to see racism as Black women's exclusive responsibility to remedy or as a social problem that did not implicate white women and how they took action in the world.[41] In other words, Slowe urged her white colleagues and their students to take up the labor of erasing the color lines that pervaded higher education and limited their profession's transformative influence.

After her talk at the University of Delaware, Slowe described her sense of its success in a follow-up letter to Blanchard. Although attendance was voluntary, Slowe reported that "almost all of the women students and many of the faculty members were present." Their interactions led her to believe that "some good seed was sown." As she noted, "a large number of the girls" lingered after the lecture, and the ensuing discussion initiated a "frank exchange of opinion." This rare conversation moved well beyond racial respectability and New Women's tendency to avoid facing the existence of the color line. Encouraged by this experience, Slowe told Blanchard, "It seems to me that this country is going to owe a big debt of gratitude to the students who are working through the YWCA for proper human relations in our land."[42]

Because Slowe pursued graduate study at Columbia University's Teachers College, the site of the first graduate program in the new profession of deaning, she had contact with many deans of women, including Amos, then the dean of women at the University of Pittsburgh. Amos served as NADW president from 1929 to 1931, and during her tenure Slowe participated as a discussion leader at the national convention and became the first African American woman to address the group.[43] Although Slowe's remarks were not racial in content—she argued that a campus's dean of women, not a student affairs office, should address the needs of women students—the context of her address certainly was. Upon her return, Howard women students honored her with a "testimonial reception," and the *Baltimore Afro-American* reported that the NADW's invitation to Slowe to speak had "[paid] to her a great tribute in recognition of her brilliance of mind and strength of character" and reflected well on women students and the campus as a whole.[44]

After the conference, Slowe thanked Amos for her role in making possible this form of visible participation. Slowe also noted a degree of resistance she encountered among the other white deans, whom she diplomatically characterized as "not as broad" and who made it challenging for a Black peer to "feel comfortable as an individual" in their presence.[45] In her response, instead of registering Slowe's specific reference to the NADW's racial dynamics, Amos emphasized what she heard as a compliment concerning her own qualities: "I would rather have it said of me that I had 'breadth of view' than almost anything in the world." Amos drew the phrase "breadth of view" not with regard to Slowe's language but in light of reading a recent description of an educated person written by Columbia University's president, Nicholas Murray Butler.[46] In personalizing and thereby decontextualizing Slowe's comments, Amos essentially delegitimized the racial import of the Black dean's words as well as her appeal to Amos for leadership among their white colleagues.

Despite their professional relationship, which extended throughout Slowe's tenure, Amos's resistance to seeing the color line became disappointingly apparent during her last of three campus visits to Howard.[47] In April 1936 she conducted a one-day institute for student campus leaders. As she would with any group of college women, Amos urged her Howard audience to take an active role in developing themselves as individuals through their academic and cocurricular experiences. Personal growth both built character and strengthened the communities to which individuals belonged. Amos insisted: "We live as individuals in groups . . . and the better the individual, the better the group."[48]

As inclusive and universal as this articulation of well-rounded growth appeared to be, it operated with racial logics. Early in the talk, Amos shared her observation that at the University of Pittsburgh, as well as other "white institutions[,] Negro students are not measuring up to the opportunities that are given to them to participate." She faulted Black students for lacking what she viewed as requisite for personal development—"you must first have a great and beautiful idea that there is something in you to be released. If I told you but you do not sense it yourself, you cannot release it, nor can some one else release it."[49] She encouraged Howard women to set an important example among HBCUs by developing and exhibiting such self-confidence themselves.

The ensuing question-and-answer session surfaced even more evidence of Amos's biased views on race. Asked specifically about the experiences of Black students at Pittsburgh, Amos repeated her assessment that these women opted out of important extracurricular growth opportunities, and she furnished the following revealing observation:

> The thing that astonishes me is that for the most part all the Negro girls seem to work on is the YWCA. *I say that if anybody discriminates against the Negro, it is that the Negro discriminates against himself.* I regret that they do not work in the WSGA [Women's Self-Government Association] as much as they might. They don't seek places on committees. Some of them make a retreat of religion. . . . I do not want religion to be a retreat for a minorities [*sic*] or people whose privileges are curtailed.[50]

Although Amos claimed this pattern of Black women's limited campus involvement was evident across colleges in the United States, her marked lack of interest in why this might be the case is curious. That is, Amos gave little consideration to the possibility of racially unwelcoming environments within those same women's organizations in which she expected Black women to participate. Amos's failure to appreciate the reasons behind the YWCA's draw for young Black women is particularly telling, as she had been a member of the National Student Council of the organization.[51] Furthermore, her office had cosponsored at least one joint event of a Black women's student group at the University of Pittsburgh and a local Black chapter of the YWCA. Finally, following a visit by Slowe to the Pittsburgh campus in May 1929, Amos had written a letter of thanks and sent greetings on behalf of "all the C.N.C.W. girls." Black women students at the University of Pittsburgh had founded the Council of Negro College Women in 1922 because of their exclusion from most student organizations outside the YWCA.[52]

Amos's unwillingness or inability to question the racial patterns she observed, however, stood apart from her active investment in addressing the gender problems of women. Thus, when asked during her 1936 visit to Howard about "getting women interested in women" so that they would support the campus's Women's League, Amos sharply focused attention on the social causes of young women's troubling lack of engagement. She asserted that behind their apparent "state of inferiority" lay an internalized belief that "no matter how poor a man may be he is better than a woman. . . . Girls for the most part would rather have the smile of the man than to stand for ideas."[53]

Given the self-development she saw at the heart of a college education, Amos then suggested ways to attract women students. Rather than fault them for their willingness to yield to men, she encouraged understanding and careful outreach: "If you want a Women's League that will attract women, do not scold the women because they do not come out. Get a program and activities that appeal to a woman. You've got to have a program."[54] Amos placed the onus of responsibility on students and deans of women to construct an extracurricular environment that would attract college women and in the process encourage them to reconsider their attitudes about self and gender. In other words, Amos believed this "woman's problem" lay within a dean's purview. In contrast, she urged no similar outreach to Black undergraduate women at white institutions and instead criticized these minoritized students for their limited and seemingly self-segregating extracurricular involvement. Such a white-centered approach to her work with women students, one all too common among many New Women deans, left Black undergraduate women vulnerable to their peers' racist exclusions and harms.

In subsequent written correspondence, Slowe referred to Amos's visit as memorable and as having provided her staff and students with "helpful . . . inspiration and information."[55] Yet, in light of Slowe's long investment in interracial cooperation and her awareness that white women drew color lines, I believe her tone did not fully speak to her concerns with white New Women deans. Her peers' minimization and neglect of Black women's realities became dramatically evident at the last NADW annual meeting of Slowe's tenure.

The fallout from the NADW's February 1937 annual convention in New Orleans starkly revealed both the ongoing racial climate of the NADW and the divergence in racial outlooks between white and Black deans. A reading of histories, as well as Slowe's contemporaneous letters to members of the NADW, demonstrate how the entrenched whiteness of the organization threatened the participation and sense of belonging that Black deans sought as they attempted to follow Slowe's urging to "do what you can to make Negro women an integral part of NADW."[56]

Telling Tales of a Meeting
White Memory and
Race-Conscious Countermemory

At the 1975 annual meeting of the NADW, Kathryn Heath, a former executive secretary, presented a brief history of the organization, including the meeting in New Orleans. Reprinted in 1976 and 1986 in the NADW's journal, the text of "Our Heritage Speaks" proudly celebrated how the profession had defined its place in higher education through the collaborative vision of its "remarkable women." In this affirming account Heath pays considerable attention to the New Orleans convention, which she had helped set up and in her history characterized as "*outrageous . . .* in a very important way" (her emphasis). What Heath identified as a problem at that conference was "the absence of our black deans," which, she quizzically acknowledged, "many in attendance perhaps had not noticed."[57]

At the time of its founding, the NADW was affiliated with the National Education Association (NEA) and as a result aligned its annual meetings with the timing and location selected by the parent organization. More than sixty educational organizations connected their conferences to the NEA's meeting of superintendents.[58] The location—New Orleans—rendered this particular NEA gathering quite attractive. In fact, by July 1, 1936, members had reserved all conference hotel rooms, a first for the organization.[59]

Part of the draw may have been the historical pageant that the NEA organized to promote "the glory of Dixie." Performed by twelve hundred schoolchildren, an apologist version of southern history unfolded in four scenes. Beginning with "the happy plantation life of the old South . . . [including] Negro voodoo dancers rais[ing] the primitive note of the Congo amidst the gentle refinement of old plantation life," the rendition then moved to the destruction of that existence through war. After celebrating

74

the South's so-called rebirth, the play concluded with "the Mardi Gras, charming echo from the Old World."[60] In addition to trafficking in Confederate nostalgia in its entertainment, the superintendents' conference also abided by the racist norms of the South. As a result, Black members were expected to use back entrances and freight elevators. Although they could attend sessions, they could not socialize and share meals with their white peers. In protest of the segregation of Black educators, several organizations, including the Julius Rosenwald Fund, a major philanthropic educational foundation, withdrew their participation.[61]

In her written history Heath referenced none of the Confederate pageantry of the NEA's conference.[62] Rather, she dwelled exclusively on the racially exclusionary terms set by the headquarters hotel for the NADW gathering and faulted its policies for proscribing the Black women deans' attendance. With exasperation Heath noted that "the only dent I could make after extensive correspondence was to get a concession that our black sisters could join in a reception or meal in a private room where no other hotel guests would see what was going on." Even under these conditions, however, the hotel would not guarantee that staff would serve the African American deans.[63]

Finding these options "too much for me to stomach" and aggrieved on behalf of "our black sisters," Heath conferred with the NADW president, Irma Voigt of Ohio University (1913–49), and together they devised a plan: they would inform the black deans of these strictures and discourage them from attending. To this end Heath enlisted Slowe's support as "that leader of her race, guider of so many young black women from around the country, and woman of so many firsts herself." Heath then telephoned Slowe for comment on a draft of the letter she intended to send to the Black deans. In her retelling Heath registered appreciation for Slowe's counsel and support and reported that Slowe "said she wouldn't change a word" in the text. Claiming that Slowe's intercession encouraged the other Black deans to "accept [the] indicated action" of her letter, Heath expressed relief that the group did "not . . . take out their justifiable outrage against the Association or me." However, she also shared a critical observation in her published account—Slowe's statement that this "was the first time the Association had been forthright about race discrimination instead of letting the black members face indignities without warning."[64]

Slowe's words were less an endorsement of the NADW's decision than at best a tempered criticism of its internal support for the injustices of racism and segregation. In fact, in an oral history interview recorded in 1971, Heath spoke again about the 1937 NADW conference in New Orleans and revealed that Slowe came to her office and used even more direct language to criticize their professional organization: "I would not change a word [in the proposed letter to the Black deans]. It's the first time we haven't been lied to." In that interview Heath also acknowledged the circumstances motivating Slowe's actions, stating that the Black dean was "a great leader of Negro women and . . . went out and did many things that she didn't want to do, but [undertook] because it was necessary to make a stand."[65] Unlike Heath's later interview, however, her written statement emphasized little of the necessity of Slowe's resistance and dwelled on how Heath felt after consulting with Slowe. With a sense of vindication for herself and the NADW, Heath then pronounced in her essay that "racial problems were resolved" before the next annual convention. She lay any acts of racism after 1937 not at the feet of the NADW but of individual hotel employees who failed to uphold the organization's policy against racial discrimination.[66] Heath's account essentially externalized racism to actors outside the NADW and kept intact a preferred image of the organization as racially innocent rather than complicit in upholding the color line.

Although Heath's recollections of the 1937 meeting comported with her broader narrative arc, which represented white New Women deans of women as "stalwarts . . . out in front fighting the discrimination battles," it is inconsistent with the facts—including Heath's own acknowledgment that most of the white deans neither registered the absence of Slowe and the other African American deans nor saw it as a problem.[67] Additionally, a summary of the meeting by Voigt, the NADW president, made no mention of the discrimination and instead touted that the success of the professional gathering was actually "enhanced by the charm of the Southland."[68] Last, and most significant, the contemporaneous correspondence and later remembrances of several Black deans contradict Heath's assertions. In short, what Heath characterized as a singular event dictated by the racist policy of a particular hotel and region, Slowe and her Black peers decried as simply one instance in a sustained pattern of disregard that fell under the radar of white sensibilities, even among those deans who, like Heath, saw themselves as acting in solidarity with "our black sisters." The letters Slowe exchanged with other Black deans, as well as with Leslie Blanchard, whom she considered a white ally, offer a strong countermemory and a corrective to Heath's valorization of the NADW.

The Black deans' accounts unsettle much about Health's recollections. A month before Heath contacted her, Slowe had voiced deep concerns about the location of the annual gathering. In a November 1936 letter to Leslie Blanchard, the former YWCA executive secretary for the National Student Council and then dean of women at Hollins College in Virginia (1935–39), Slowe was keen to express her reservations about the upcoming conference. She explained: "I am not at all sure that I shall be at the meeting in New Orleans, because I am not sure that I can attend the meeting with that degree of self-respect which, as an individual and an American, I should have. . . . The conditions which exist in New Orleans exist practically in every place in the South and for that reason educational organizations, in my judgment, should stay out of the South."[69]

Slowe's references to her self-respect and rights as an American were reflections of her New Negro Women sensibilities. Perceiving herself as an equal, she rejected a lesser kind of membership in the NADW or in society as a whole. Moreover, she highlighted how tiresome and disappointing she found the New Orleans situation and insisted that educators in particular carried an ethical responsibility to protest segregation. She also offered a comparison that further revealed the NADW's troubling practice of accommodation of the color line, telling Blanchard, "This is the same old question that you and I fought together on in the Young Women's Christian Association, so we are quite familiar with it."[70]

In her own response two weeks later, Blanchard conveyed a shared understanding of Slowe's principled objections to, and hurt resulting from, the racist exclusion and the NADW's moral cowardice. Blanchard also recognized the gravity of the situation. She approached it with a sense of responsibility—"I appreciate fully the problem which it presents to us both"—and evidenced an ongoing commitment to interracial progress, mentioning that she "confront[ed] day by day in my work here in Virginia . . . the questions on which we have thought together in the Y.W.C.A." Although Blanchard planned to attend the New Orleans NADW meeting, she vowed "to make every effort through the membership to raise these issues and attempt to make progress on it." Having spent most of her career with the YWCA, Blanchard was new to the NADW and its avoidance of racial issues. Significantly, she echoed Slowe's assessment that the NADW was less racially progressive than the YWCA. As Blanchard noted, "Apparently we are dealing with a group in which this question has not come to a focus." From their years of working toward interracial community at the YWCA, Blanchard met Slowe's racial witnessing with solidarity, not doubt or evasion: "I have not abandoned any of my convictions on this point and the problem of working in a new social relationship is a continuously keen one for me."[71]

Slowe also registered her concerns directly with the NADW leadership. On December 3, 1936, she penned a letter to Voigt, inquiring "whether or not the Executive Committee of our Association has done anything to make it possible for all members, without regard to race, to attend the meeting and keep their self-respect." Slowe then shared her knowledge of the segregationist practices of New Orleans and highlighted the affront to peers of color, telling Voigt, "Of course, no self-respecting person could attend a meeting under these conditions." Slowe explained her view that the NADW itself ought to stand with other organizations in opposition and not "lend its aid or its influence in perpetuating customs which are an insult to a national body of American citizens." As a matter of principle, Slowe insisted that it was the responsibility of the "Executive Committee . . . [to] take this matter up with the N.E.A. and . . . not cease its protest until the matter is settled in the right way."[72] Slowe's papers contain no response from Voigt.

Three weeks later Slowe and Heath communicated about the New Orleans convention, and in early January 1937 Heath sent the NADW's institutional letter to Slowe and the other Black deans. Written in a dispassionate tone, the letter presented the organization as a powerless and neutral bystander to societal racism: the "N.A.D.W. accepts the convention city chosen by the Department of Superintendence of the National Education Association." Characterizing the situation as regrettable and in conflict with the fact that the NADW "draws no racial distinctions" among its members, the NADW's letter sidestepped its responsibility, concluding with the statement that "The Association deeply regrets the segregation system which has prompted the writing of this letter."[73]

Despite the courteous tone of letters that Slowe and Heath exchanged after the convention, Heath's overtures at reconciliation resolved little for

RACE WORK IS WOMEN'S WORK

Slowe or the other African American deans. During the week of the actual NADW meeting, Howard alumna Hilda Davis, then the director of women's activities at Talladega College, wrote to Slowe about her own letter-writing campaign of protest. She expressed the hope that "perhaps a show-down will come with [the] N.E.A. Dean Blanding, Leslie Blanchard, and several other deans are planning to make an issue of these conditions. I believe that something positive will result."[74] In response Slowe also pointed out that the work to be done required white women's efforts and noted that she was "very glad that some of the white deans were willing to take up the matter."[75]

The challenge to Slowe's self-respect—occurring at the end of fourteen years of engagement with the NADW—remained an ongoing part of Black deans' experiences with the organization. In 1979, four years after Heath's initial presentation of her history at an NADW annual conference, a group of Black current and former student affairs officers—including deans of women—organized a panel titled "Our Living History: Reminiscences of Black Participation in NAWDAC" (National Association of Women Deans, Administrators, and Counselors).[76] The panelists assembled out of a sense of urgency rooted in their fear that "this part of the history of NAWDAC would be lost [if those who] knew it firsthand did not share this information."[77] Clearly, the organizational perspective in circulation left troubling gaps in the accounts of events that the Black deans had experienced, rendering the official narrative incomplete, if not fraudulent, to them.

What these early Black members of the NADW revealed was that the indignities and exclusions of 1937 were not restricted to that particular meeting in New Orleans but were a regular aspect of being "sister deans" to the white members. Most of the panelists had served in the NADW after Slowe, and their memories collectively referenced the racial dynamics of the organization across five decades, from the early 1930s into the 1970s. Davis joined the organization in 1933 and confirmed that the New Orleans convention was not a singular incident but part of "the pattern year after year in city after city, even in large cities, like Chicago, New York, and Washington."[78] Although Black deans were allowed to attend the conferences, they typically could not stay in the headquarters hotels and thus had to secure accommodations either with Black families or at Black-owned properties and boardinghouses. Davis also affirmed that Slowe had not been a silent witness to this pattern. For several years Slowe had "publicly deplored the conditions under which the Negro members could participate in NADW's national conventions" through discussions with the executive board and at conference business meetings. Despite the "formal protest[s]" of the Black deans, by Davis's estimation it took another twenty years for the NADW to decide not to gather in racially segregated cities.[79]

Ruth Brett, director of counseling and academic advising at Morgan State College and a former student of Hilda Davis's, joined the NADW in 1939. Her account, published in 1986, spoke to the emotional toll of the NADW's denial of full participation to all its members. When she attended her first convention in 1940, she "wept inside," not just for herself—she could access neither lodging nor service at the St. Louis conference hotel—but for another Black dean who "found the accommodations so inadequate that she left and never returned to NADW." Brett further revealed that the problem of segregation extended beyond the conference headquarters hotels to the organization itself. Throughout her career she and the other Black deans were "conspicuous by their absence in most conference programs." Moreover, task forces continued into the late 1970s and failed to understand the problem of low membership numbers among racial minority deans as well as their grievances at being expected to accept less than complete membership rights in the NADW. Although she acknowledged the support of some white deans within and outside the NADW, Brett remained a participating member by continuing to operate on the "faith that eventually I would feel that I was part of NADW." She concluded that while she did eventually experience professional belonging, "I know that many other minority members do not; and too many have felt that it was not worth bothering about."[80]

Dean Edna M. Calhoun confirmed that from her first NADW conference in 1955, eighteen years after what Heath had termed the New Orleans outrage, racial problems continued within the organization.[81] Lucille Johnson Piggott, dean of student affairs at North Carolina Agricultural and Technical State University, acknowledged the presence of "a strong band of white deans who tried successfully to persuade their colleagues to eliminate prejudices" yet also pointed out a prevailing refusal within the organization "to stop playing games against the minority members of the Association."[82] These countermemories of the Black deans locate the problem of racism squarely within the NADW, not external to it, as Heath had suggested.

Conclusion

On its own, the NADW was not a leading organization in the promotion of racial inclusion. As the historian Kelly Sartorius writes, "The strongest thread tying deans of women to racial activism rested in their cooperation with the Young Women's Christian Association."[83] Despite the racist views evidenced among Slowe's white NADW peers into the last year of her career, there are some indications that her vision and person effected some changes. In a reference to the 1940 NADW conference, Ruth Brett described Voigt, the organization's president during the 1937 convention, as "one of the most courageous and determined women I have known." Brett recounted how Voigt had made a public statement against segregation by walking with a few Black deans "through the hotel lobby, through the dining room to a separate room where we had lunch with her and Sarah Blanding, who was president."[84] It is not clear what changed Voigt's thinking about how racial segregation impacted the Black NADW members.

There are also intriguing suggestions of a heightened racial awareness emergent in Thyrsa Amos. In addition to attending Slowe's funeral in October 1937, Amos hosted a luncheon as well as a memorial service for Slowe at the University of Pittsburgh's Women's Center during the NACW's April 1938 annual meeting.[85] Amos's tribute was titled "Lucy Diggs Slowe: A Pioneer in the Education of Women."[86] In a remembrance of Slowe submitted for an issue of the 1938 *National Association of College Women Journal*, Amos acknowledged that few of her relationships with women extended across the color line: "[Lucy Slowe] is the first Negro woman leader whom I came to know well, and with whom I could talk freely about the constructive relationship of our two races."[87] Amos's words appear to recognize the limits of her own racial knowledge and the value of Slowe's perspectives on interracial possibilities. Furthermore, in hosting the NACW on her campus, Amos seemed to appreciate Slowe's importance both to the deans of women movement and to the Black alumnae whose organizations—including the NACW and the National Association of Women's Deans and Advisers of Colored Schools, which Slowe founded—existed in large part because they experienced ongoing forms of exclusion from New Women's professional associations. However, Amos's statement also touted her own growth and personal betterment in the context of Slowe's inspiring qualities instead of expressing a commitment to scrutinizing her own racial attitudes and actions. In describing a connection with Slowe that existed "above race," Amos's tribute created a space of transcendence, a world in which race did not matter, a comfortable environment for a white woman to occupy.[88] As a result, Amos's comments did not challenge the NADW's dominant imaginary of itself and its white members as good, inclusive, and committed to women.

Within the NADW the lack of consistent support among white women for Slowe's vision of mutuality reinforced much of her knowledge of the United States as a white-dominated society with a deep strain of anti-Blackness that was maintained, not insignificantly, by a majority of white men and women. Because of white women's problematic support for the color line, the NADW failed to meet Slowe's aspiration that New Negro Women and New Women would partner in cultivating a new world—that of a racially inclusive democracy.

CHAPTER 4

OUR DEAN, OUR SELVES
THE PERSECUTION AND DEFENSE
OF A NEW NEGRO WOMAN

On May 15, 1933 when you were President of the Trustee Board of Howard
University you said to Miss Slowe that you had been told by one of the Trustees
of Howard University that there would be 'no peace at Howard University as
long as she was on the campus'! . . . Although Lucy D. Slowe has gone from
the campus, is there peace there? . . . There is another reason for the perpetual
turmoil at Howard than the presence there of Howard's distinguished alumna
and former Dean of Women, Lucy D. Slowe—a great woman of our race.

—**Mary Burrill to Dr. Abraham Flexner, former chair of
the Howard board of trustees, May 2, 1938**

College presidents have never been put on the spot like deans of women;
in fact, they sometimes make the spots for the women deans.

— **Lucy Diggs Slowe, quoted in the *Baltimore Afro-American*, December 1, 1934**

At a 1936 meeting of the National Association of Women's Deans and Advisors of Colored Schools at Wilberforce University, Slowe recalled her
first days as dean at Howard. An administrative colleague, a man, offered
the following greeting: "I am so glad you are coming up here because there
will be some one on the campus at night after all the rest of us have gone
home." Taken aback by his words but recovering quickly in her response,
Slowe corrected his assumption about being a "campus housekeeper" or
"lady cop," explaining, "But you know I shall not be on the campus either. . . . Because when you go home I shall go home too."[1] Although her
retelling is humorous, Slowe's archive of memos and letters reveals that
she encountered entrenched sexist misperceptions of her role and work
throughout her tenure at her alma mater.

83

In addition to confronting the racism of white deans of women, Slowe challenged the heteropatriarchal gender structure of Howard University. Given her involvement in the extracurricular lives of women, she understood her vantage point to be unique as well as necessary. She saw herself as "a constant vigilant and wise observer of what the college is really doing for students."[2] That Slowe "remained unapologetic and unwavering" in her promotion of progressive gender relations within the Black community was the source of much friction between her and the university's administration, certain faculty, and members of the board of trustees.[3] As she understood and repeatedly articulated, a dean of women was a necessary advocate for women students whose needs and presence were at risk of neglect within men-centered and men-administered institutions, whether historically Black or "persistently white."[4] However, she was not alone in her struggles. Other New Negro Women saw themselves in Slowe, and in their own letter-writing campaigns and voiceful advocacy, they challenged the vilification of her work and person. Embracing the proposition that Black women mattered, and putting the weight of their support behind Slowe's vision of living more abundantly, Howard women students, in particular, rallied against the force of men-dominated power structures that dictated the terms of Black women's respectability and the prerogatives of Black masculinity.

The New Negro
A Patriarchal Racial and Educational Agent

By the time of Slowe's hiring as her alma mater's dean of women in 1922, the limitations of using respectability for renegotiating Black people's status within society were alarmingly evident. Irrespective of African Americans' self-sufficient behavior and commitment to American values, whites refused to grant them the protections, opportunities, and recognitions of full citizenship. The virulent anti-Black racism of both legalized segregation and the spread of lynching as an unpunished "ritual of white power" belied the promises of Emancipation and Reconstruction.[5] Along with a growing social discontent—evident in the Black soldiers who had returned from providing patriotic service in the First World War, the migration of southern Blacks to northern cities for physical safety and economic opportunity, and the immigration of West Indians—a new social movement was born. Self-proclaimed New Negro men rejected nineteenth-century codes of respectability and insisted on their right to embody a patriarchal form of self-determination within Black communities, politics, intellectual production, and the creative arts.[6]

The philosopher Alain Locke (1885–1954), Slowe's Howard University colleague and contemporary, powerfully articulated the New Negro's distinction from the Reconstruction-era ideology of respectability. In the lead essay for his 1925 anthology, *The New Negro*, Locke proclaimed an end to "the Old Negro" and his offensively feminine posture of deference and dependence. As Locke emphasized, the New Negro "lays aside the status of a beneficiary and ward for that of a collaborator and participant in American civilization."[7] In pursuit of an "assertive but cultured" masculine agency, New Negro adherents valorized a "driving quest for self-determination" to offset the effects of both slavery and respectability.[8] Consequently, in their efforts to "man the race," New Negro Men assumed leadership of both Black families and other social institutions.[9]

The New Negro's abandonment of servile "social mimicry" in pursuit of "true social [and] self-understanding" offered little recognition of Black women as political, intellectual, or cultural equals.[10] As the liberation of Black men as men took center stage in the racial strivings of African Americans, Black women were to complement respectability's self-surveillance with their visible "subordination to strong, benevolent, capable black patriarchs."[11] Consequently, the New Negro's counterpart was not a peer but a deferential race woman expected to occupy a parallel yet "invisible talented tenth," a space of achievement in which Black women focused their efforts on strengthening Black men–centered notions of marriage, family, and community.[12]

In her own contribution to Locke's anthology, the activist-educator Elise Johnson McDougald drew a revealing parallel between "the modern Negro mother . . . [and] the much extolled, yet pitiable black mammy of slavery days": both maternal figures experienced a tension between a desire to be self-directed and a competing, socially normalized expectation to be "loyal and tender." As a result, McDougald observed, "on the whole the Negro woman's feminist efforts are directed chiefly toward the realization of the equality of the races, the sex struggle assuming the subordinate place." As McDougald expressed in an earlier version of this essay, the struggle of Black women amid New Negro Men continued to be a "double task" against both white racism and intraracial sexism.[13]

A Dean, Not a Matron
A Question of Residence

As a new profession developed by women, deaning suffered from a perception that it was a lesser undertaking than other administrative work in higher education. Slowe acknowledged as much in a letter to Abraham Flexner, chair of Howard's board, in 1933. "Unfortunately," she wrote, "some people conceive of the Dean of Women as a dormitory supervisor or matron whereas she is forced by the nature of her work to be an administrative officer with university-wide duties."[14] During her tenure and through her work with the National Association of College Women (NACW), Slowe attempted to correct this persistent mischaracterization shared by many of the men who were college presidents and trustees. As conceptualized by Slowe, the NACW was an accountability organization working to shift HBCUs' operations from their nineteenth-century founding in principles of respectability to twentieth-century ideals of equal worth and opportunity. Key to this modernization was the incorporation of the position and office of dean of women. To this end, NACW members visited HBCU campuses and administered follow-up questionnaires focused on assessing institutional progress toward previously stated goals of equity for women.[15]

In her fifteen years as dean, Slowe served under two Howard presidents. The last white leader of the university, J. Stanley Durkee (1918–26), hired her, and she experienced the historic appointment of the institution's first Black president, Mordecai Wyatt Johnson (1926–60). Despite important differences between them, the two men shared a view of her as a semi-professional. As a result, both took actions Slowe interpreted as deeply regressive and invalidating of her standing, such as singling her out among her university peers to require her residence on campus as a condition of continued employment.

Slowe initially was confident that she could maintain a private home off campus because she had negotiated this specific point with Durkee. In a follow-up letter she sent him to clarify "the several agreements cov-

**Lucy Diggs Slowe
and Mary Burrill in
their backyard, 1932.**
Courtesy of the Moorland-
Spingarn Research Center,
Howard University Archives,
Howard University,
Washington, D.C.

ered . . . for your verification and endorsement," Slowe highlighted the
terms most important to her: her faculty position as a professor of English
in the School of Education and the administrative title she would hold, her
salary, and the staffing for her office. She also included this explicit statement: "I shall not be required to live on the campus."[16] Along with increasing numbers of her white dean counterparts, Slowe expected a clear break
from expectations she would have to act as a matron and saw herself solely
as an administrative professional.

In addition to recognizing her administrative standing, Slowe's residence off campus allowed her to maintain her private life with Mary "Mamie" Burrill (1881–1946), who taught English and drama at Dunbar High

87

School in Washington, D.C., from 1907 to 1945.[17] An educator and playwright, Burrill had met Slowe in 1912, and the two women began sharing a home while Slowe was principal at Shaw Junior High School (1919–22). They remained life partners for twenty-five years, until Slowe's death in 1937.[18]

Soon after accepting the offer to serve as Howard's first dean of women, Slowe and Burrill purchased a home together at 1256 Kearney Street in the Brookland neighborhood of northeast Washington, D.C. The two-and-a-half story Queen Anne structure was built in 1890.[19] Landscaped with fifty rose bushes, the property included six mature maple trees and a rock garden containing "many different kinds of flowers in it."[20] The house was a five-minute drive or a twenty-five-minute walk from the university, and its location did not impair Slowe's ability to keep regular work hours of 9:00 a.m. to 4:30 p.m., to return to campus for evening meetings, or to have student groups gather at her house "several times a week."[21] Her residence extended the affirming geography she had established on campus for women students. Reflecting on her many visits to Slowe's home, the alumna Valarie O'Mega Justiss characterized the dean as an attentive and even indulgent hostess who could engage lightheartedly with the students: "While she made cocoa and fudge, we raided the ice box as though we were in our own homes. We concluded the evening only after we had sampled all her jelly, tasted rather generously all left-overs, quarreled over who was to have some particular delicacy that she remembered was in an out-of-way place and then as though that were not enough, we tramped through the house on a personally conducted tour of inspection."[22] In this space that was open and familiar to students, Slowe hosted meetings of the Women's League cabinet as well as annual garden parties for graduating senior women.[23]

Despite the initial agreement Slowe had reached with Durkee regarding the terms of her appointment, at the end of her third year in late June 1925, a committee of the board of trustees decided to move her to campus. Perhaps prompted by Slowe's own insistence that such an action broke with current professional practice, Durkee wrote to Mina Kerr, who had served as president of the National Association of Deans of Women (NADW) from 1920 to 1923 and who was its current executive secretary, to solicit her "opinion regarding the advisability of deans of women living on the campus."[24] Kerr responded the same day she received Durkee's letter and recounted a brief history of the profession. She acknowledged an important evolution in the work during the previous ten years: whereas at the turn of the century, from 1900 to 1915, "practically all deans lived on the campus in the residence halls and had charge of the minutest details of the social and home life of the students," with the rise of the profession "presidents and boards of trustees have come to realize that women deans like men deans, women professors like men professors, do better work on the whole for students when they have some separate home life of their own, some time away from their work for rest, study and thought."[25] In a brief three paragraphs, Kerr alerted Durkee to a point that many campus presidents never completely appreciated or recognized—that deans of women were administrative professionals, due the same respect and work conditions extended to men of their training and rank.

Durkee eventually agreed to honor his original housing agreement with Slowe. Yet his power, and that of other men administrators, to challenge and attempt to alter what Slowe and other deans of women considered to be a basic term of their appointments served as an uncomfortable reminder of their vulnerable professional standing on men-run campuses. Although this particular attempt to deprofessionalize Slowe's office failed, the question of her housing would resurface forcefully under the subsequent administration of Johnson, a last step in his protracted campaign to humiliate her and discredit her work on campus.

Standing Up for "My Girls"
Dean Slowe and Professor Mills

After six decades of campus leadership by white men, in 1926 Mordecai Wyatt Johnson (1890–1976) was named president of Howard University. An ordained Baptist minister and educator, he had earned degrees from Atlanta Baptist College, the University of Chicago, Rochester Theological Seminary, and Harvard University. During his thirty-four-year tenure, Johnson expanded Howard's faculty and student body and improved its academic standing.[26] Despite these laudable achievements, he was not an advocate for women's campus life, as Slowe envisioned it. Her philosophy of living more abundantly and her New Negro Woman assertions of voice and equality ran afoul of Johnson's conservative gender ideology. Consequently, using the power of his office, Johnson engaged in what Slowe's many supporters among alumnae, deans of women, and the Black press collectively viewed as his unwarranted and malicious persecution of a committed daughter of Howard.[27]

Slowe's October 1922 introduction of the New Howard Woman and her invocation of the need for a new masculinity among Howard men would not have been lost on Clarence H. Mills, who in four years would effect a major turning point in her career at Howard. With a bachelor's degree from Dartmouth and a master's from Harvard, Mills joined the Howard faculty as an instructor in French the same year Slowe returned to her alma mater.[28]

In January 1927, during the second academic quarter of the Johnson presidency, the mother of a woman student wrote to Slowe about Mills, expressing concern about his use of "improper and sometimes vulgar language" and its creation of an uncomfortable learning environment for her daughter and peers. Taking this parent's complaints seriously, Slowe quickly reached out to Mills personally. After coming to an apparent understanding, in which—according to Slowe—he expressed thanks for her intervention and the avoidance of the mother's lodging a formal complaint with Johnson, Mills engaged in an about-face and sent what Slowe later described in a memo as "one of the vilest letters that any woman could possibly receive from a man."[29]

Mills's invective revealed much about Howard's patriarchal gender structure and the institution's beliefs about color, class, and heteronormativity. Writing on January 11, 1927, Mills addressed Slowe in a highly emotional, seemingly hastily typed letter, in which he misspelled her last name and referred to her not by title but as "Madam." As he lashed out with unmitigated patriarchal arrogance, he impugned both her person and the position she held. He accused her of participating in a mulatto conspiracy against darker-skinned yet more qualified faculty, and he threatened to sue her personally. He also attacked her character and that of the women students in her charge: "You forget that you are merely the Dean of Women and not the custodian of morals of the male teachers of Howard University. It is my opinion if you had something to do and two classes to teach as the other Deans, you would'nt [sic] hear so much. And if what I can hear about your character is true, you would be summarily dismissed from Howard University and made hall matron of the principal whore houses in Washington."[30] In this unvarnished act of "gender disciplining," Mills charged her with "prosecuting lies" against men faculty members and asserted that her role as dean of women left her with insufficient work and the leisure to take up hearsay.[31] Furthermore, he characterized her sharing a household with Mary Burrill as immoral. His multiple assaults marked her as a woman (not a man), a matron (not a scholar), and as queer (not heterosexual). In his view each of these qualities invalidated any charges she might bring against him.

Rather than respond with silence or cower in the face of his attack, Slowe enlisted the support of men administrators, and one accompanied her to a meeting with Johnson. In her "Memorandum on the Mills Case," which she wrote in May 1933, she recounted her insistence to the president that "Prof. Mills should leave the University immediately for he was unfit to teach the students and unfit to associate with the faculty." In an attempt to avoid negative publicity for the university and seeing merit in her concerns, the administrators decided on this course of action: Mills would formally apologize to Slowe, finish the quarter, and then "be quietly let out of the University."[32]

Pursuant to this agreement, Mills sent a carefully worded one-paragraph retraction to "Dean Slowe." Reflecting a level of care absent in his attack two days earlier, he both specified and capitalized the time of "TEN THIRTY A.M." He claimed to have written the first letter "under the pressure of a severe mental strain bordering on a nervous breakdown" and implored her to "be magnanimous enough to return the said letter to me in the presence of such authorized persons as you may designate so that I destroy it and offer to you a verbal apology which is certainly due you."[33]

Despite this admission of wrongdoing and the corrective action agreed upon by the administrators, the university retained Mills through not only the winter quarter but the spring term as well. Slowe accurately viewed this decision as rewarding rather than censuring Mills's libelous behavior toward her and the women students, and she gave Johnson an ultimatum: "I told him that either Prof. Mills would go or I would go. I said that if he was so sick that he did not know what he was doing when he insulted me and the students of the University, he was too sick to remain on the staff. If he was not sick, he was unfit to remain."[34]

Although Mills's supporters then pressured Slowe to soften her assessment of the situation, she emphasized in her 1933 memorandum the impossibility of doing so: "I could not do this and keep my self-respect, or the re-

spect of worthwhile people who might know about the case." In addition
to allowing Mills to complete the school year, the university granted him
a subsequent leave of absence at half pay, which he used to complete his
doctoral degree at the University of Chicago. As Slowe incisively observed
in her memo, "He could not have been very sick to have been able to do
this."[35]

Johnson's heteropatriarchal views about women were a major point of
contention between him and Slowe, and his handling of the Mills case was
their first serious clash. With the benefit of hindsight, she summarized in
the same 1933 memo that "from the time this case happened down to the
present, I have not had the cordial support of the President." Seven years
into her work in his administration, she found Johnson willfully ignorant
about her efforts and profession: "He has never sympathetically studied
the real work of the Dean of Women. . . . He confuses her with a matron.
He seldom comes to any function sponsored by the Department of the
Dean of Women, and cannot have first hand knowledge of her work. I
have tried in every way to correct this but can get no co-operation from the
President."[36] For Slowe's part, Johnson's disparagement of her reflected a
fundamental conflict between his paternalistic view of women and the advocacy she saw as central to her campus role. And in their subsequent correspondence, her voice was insistent and righteous because of how little
Johnson recognized her world in his own.

On the archival copy of Slowe's memo, Mary Burrill vehemently de-
nounced Johnson as a "petty President reared and *educated not* for Education, but for the *Ministry*" (emphasis hers).[37] Furthermore, in 1939, as she
organized the dean's papers, Burrill composed her own note about Mills's
"infamous letter." Far from an exaggeration, Burrill's reference to a persecution that was "continuous and heartless" was consistent with the contemporaneous assessments of others—including Howard women students
and alumnae, Slowe's white dean peers, and the Black press—regarding
Johnson's unfair and humiliating treatment of the most well-known expert
in Black women's higher education.[38]

The Persecution Begins

At the start of the 1930–31 academic year, Johnson elected to remove the
dean of women as well as the dean of men from the university council and

its weekly meetings. Slowe viewed this decision as wholly ill-advised given her charge. As she wrote to the president, "To cut off the Deans who direct the student in his extra classroom life from those who direct his inside classroom life is like cutting an arm from the body and telling the former to function."[39] She asserted that "women students ought to have a special representative among the administrative officers, for their interests are somewhat different from those of men students."[40] It was precisely this vantage point and role that Johnson refused to acknowledge and value in his administration.

Neither Slowe nor the dean of men was reinstated on the administrative council. But she was singled out for further disparagements throughout the remainder of her tenure. During the spring term following the opening of the Women's Campus in the fall of 1931, Kelly Miller, the sociologist and former dean of the College of Arts and Sciences, wrote to Johnson to suggest naming one of the three new dorms after her. Describing Slowe as "the leading alumna of Howard University . . . [and] the most effective and influential colored woman now functioning in the sphere of higher education," Miller further reminded Johnson that during ten years of Slowe's leadership, the Women's Department (Slowe's office and the activities it supported on behalf of Howard undergraduate women) had earned a "place and recognition in the sisterhood of American female and coeducational colleges."[41] Slowe's campus achievements included the Women's Dinner, which was entering its second decade, and the establishment of a number of mentoring programs. Furthermore, since 1930 she had offered, through the university's department of education, an undergraduate course in deaning to introduce a younger generation to the work.[42] However, in one of the many affronts she would experience during his administration, Johnson refused to grant Slowe the recognition she deserved. In his response to Miller, Johnson "advised that it was against the policy of the university to name a structure after a living person," even though several other buildings—including the library, science hall, and the university itself—all carried the names of men who were not deceased when the buildings were dedicated.[43]

Johnson's attempts to delegitimize Slowe's campus standing took full effect at the end of the 1932–33 school year when he and the board of trustees issued several decisions to dismantle the Women's Department. Eighteen months after the opening of the dorms of the Women's Campus, Johnson

Slowe among men Howard administrators, November 1930.
Courtesy of Scurlock Studio Records, Archives Center,
National Museum of American History, Smithsonian Institution.

informed Slowe of his upcoming decision to transfer management of all student housing—women's and men's—to the university treasurer.[44] Although he professed to be following the institution's bylaws, it was more likely that he was motivated to find a clause that would allow him to return to a structure of control that predated the women's dorms and Slowe's hiring as dean of women. Claiming financial hardship, the board then pressed for a drastic reduction in Slowe's office personnel, including the firing of the women's doctor, the graduate dietician, and one of the two dormitory directors. As a result, all that remained of the women's program staff was Slowe and an assistant, who also oversaw a dormitory. This gutting of the Women's Department, as Slowe passionately expressed in a letter to the board of trustees, "destroyed, in one day, practically everything that I had built up over a period of eleven years."[45] Last—and most devastating and humiliating—the board ordered her to live in campus housing.

As I examined in chapter 2, the Women's Campus was designed to be an alternative, women-controlled geography focused on promoting college women's development. Given this intentional and necessary function,

Slowe's office staff was deeply troubled by Johnson's abrupt placement of the dormitories under the treasurer's control. Just months later, Joanna Houston, a Howard alumna and Slowe's assistant, couched criticism of the management shift within her 1932–33 annual report to the dean of women: "Those of us who assisted with the initiation of life on this side of the campus, and who have invested ourselves and our means unstintedly [sic] in the program because of the possibilities we saw in it, cannot sit quietly by and see what was set up as a cultural center for Negro women—the only one of its kind—turned into a commercial center where all culture is disregarded.[46] Striking a similarly aggrieved tone in her own memo to the treasurer, Slowe described the dorms as no longer constituting a Women's Campus but as fast becoming a "public Commons" and a hotel that hosted mixed-gender groups of visiting students.[47] In a letter to Slowe, Houston characterized the atmosphere of the dorms as approaching a "men's club."[48]

Women students were not quiet about their own outrage in regard to the loss of control of their space. In a memo to Slowe they described a grossly substandard operation in the dining hall that included "ill-prepared . . . cold . . . indigestible" meals, insufficient utensils, and inefficient and discourteous service. They also detailed a wholly unacceptable level of food handling that included "bread stale, butter finger-printed, hair in foods, straw and rope found in foods; spinach and other leafy vegetables gritty from apparently lack of *wash*" (emphasis theirs). The authors of the memo concluded that what was supposed to be "an atmosphere of culture has deteriorated into a literal hovel."[49] Slowe and her supporters correctly understood the shift in supervision to be an insult—not only to the women students who deserved a space of their own but to her as the architect of an environment designed to cultivate the New Howard Woman well beyond compliance with black men's chauvinism.

Women students also protested the loss of personnel for the Women's Department. In a move that demonstrated courage, political savvy, and their identification with New Negro Women expectations of equality, they shared directly with the *Baltimore Afro-American* a May 2, 1933, letter of protest addressed to Johnson and the board because the women "wanted no garbled account of what they were doing."[50] Signed by the president of the Women's League and eleven other students on behalf of their aggrieved peers, the letter was a demand that the women's doctor be retained. The students recalled that the appointment of the women's physician, Dr. Dorothy Boulding Ferebee, had initially been made "in answer to a protest raised by mothers and daughters" concerning administration of the mandatory physical examination by the physician who was a man. Because the trustees claimed that the firing of the women's doctor was an issue of economy even as they chose to retain the full-time services of the men's physician, the students provided an equitable alternative: both medical professionals should become half-time employees. The twelve signatories also underscored that "the majority of women students" on campus shared their outrage.[51]

In his fiery response to the young women, Flexner, the board chair, presented them with an ultimatum—they could either accept the trustees' decision or transfer from the college.[52] Outraged by his arrogant dismissal of their concerns, the women students addressed a second letter to him and insisted on his resignation. In its Washington, D.C., edition of May 13, 1933, the *Afro-American* newspaper quoted excerpts in which the women students expressed their indignation at Flexner's condescending attitude. In an article under the headline "Howard Women Rebuke Trustee Board Head," the women maintained that they were within their rights as students to "question the action of the trustees." Again led by the president of the Women's League, the students emphasized that they had already secured the signatures of three hundred women and had solicited alumnae support for their protest.[53]

What the Howard women students accurately read in Flexner's letter was a nineteenth-century attitude of patronizing white benevolence that they publicly decried as an affront to their twentieth-century, New Negro Woman sensibilities. They contrasted their understanding of Howard's mission to foster Black leadership with Flexner's contemptuous tone, which they rejected as consistent with "a regime of . . . slavery."[54] Despite their appeal and its backing by the Black press, in June 1933 the board discontinued Dr. Ferebee's services.

Writing to Slowe directly, Flexner referred to the protesting college women as a "crowd of girls" and chastised their behavior. To him, the dean's support for their actions provided "no stronger evidence of the importance of your being on the grounds and getting their confidence in such wise [sic] that they will not take such silly steps without conference with you."[55] Concerned that her work was being misrepresented, Slowe addressed a follow-up letter to him and included letters of support she had solicited from other deans and from students. Because of her belief that her difficulties with the Johnson administration began with the Mills situation, she also provided copies of their correspondence and her own explanatory memo about the case. Despite this documentation, Johnson and Flexner regarded her outspokenness and refusal to concede to gendered practices a problem they hoped that further program reductions and mandating her residence on university grounds would resolve. As Slowe later recalled, it was during a phone call on May 15, 1933, that Flexner conveyed to her another trustee's caustic comment that "there would be no peace at Howard University as long as I was on the campus."[56]

Howard alumnae quickly recognized the deep meaning of the trustees' order for Slowe to reside on campus. It was an effort to demote Slowe to a matron and subject the women students to her supervision. Again, as with the firing of the Women's Department staff, Howard women took action. Alumnae wrote directly to the trustees about this "attempt to take from the position of Dean of Women some of its administrative status," adding their awareness that "the Dean of Men has been left undisturbed in his own home . . . [which] is being interpreted by many as sex discrimination which is not in keeping with the spirit of the day."[57] In her own letter to the trustees, a former instructor at Howard placed the housing decision in the context of the university's standing in higher education, writing that the unfair decision had "implications, not only to Howard men and women, but to colored men and women everywhere."[58] All of Slowe's work to recognize Black women students as capable, responsible, and valued individuals was being compromised by what she regarded as the Johnson administration's vindictive action to put her—and by extension all the women who looked up to Slowe—under paternalistic university control.[59]

The humiliation of the housing decision only grew when in late June 1933, Johnson advised Slowe which house he intended for her to occupy. In a follow-up letter to him, she pointedly detailed the actual condition of the residence: "The house is situated on an unpaved, blind street next to the University dump. Trash and dirt are hauled to this dump every day and burned. . . . A more unsightly, unattractive and unsanitary place could not have been chosen as a suitable residence for the Dean of Women of Howard University."[60] The Black press continued its support of Dean Slowe, and in July 1933 an unnamed "special correspondent" from the *Baltimore*

Afro-American took up her cause and wrote a series of articles characterizing the board of trustees' decision to force her to reside on campus as "purely and solely punitive."[61] Fearing an attempt by the Howard administration to beautify the structure, the journalist took pictures of the dwelling offered to Slowe. Furthermore, the writer compared Slowe's mistreatment to medieval torture and concluded that, even if justified, Howard's actions toward Slowe violated all tenets of fairness. The reporter then landed on the real cause of the university's cruel action: it was a "technique for the punishing of a woman who apparently does not ride on the bandwagon."[62]

In an attempt to protect her name and work, Slowe reached out to the vice president of the interracial board of trustees, George Williamson Crawford, a lawyer from New Haven, Connecticut.[63] He was not a member of the executive committee that had decided to move her to campus, and Slowe hoped he would be sympathetic to her situation.[64] Crawford, a graduate of Talladega College and Yale Law School, and a protégé of W. E. B. Du Bois's, had sat on the Howard University board since 1926.[65] Slowe acknowledged to him her reluctance to contact trustees directly out of concern that she would be perceived as a nuisance, but she also maintained that "in order to defend myself and to defend the interests of the women students," she was left with no choice but to do so.[66]

Throughout the summer of 1933, Slowe kept Crawford abreast of her situation even though his responses largely reflected indifference to her case. Her persistence reflected her desperation. As she explained in her final letter to him, dated August 17, 1933, "It seems as soon as I get over one hurdle, [President Johnson] sets up another. . . . It looks as if the President has created this dilemma for me to force me into the dormitory where he thinks a dean of women should be. He does not want the Dean of Women at Howard to have any administrative standing; he has always wanted her to be a matron." Lacking a man advocate to intervene on her behalf, Slowe believed that Johnson felt empowered to threaten and demean her. On this last point she offered a revealing elaboration: "Maybe I have no right to say these things to you, but I must trust somebody and I don't know whom to turn to. There is not a single man in my own family to confer with, and no woman can cope with this situation alone. If Dr. Slowe—my brother— were living, things would have been very different."[67]

Slowe's late brother was the Philadelphia dentist William Myers Slowe,

a 1900 graduate of Howard University's Medical Department, an honor-
ably discharged first lieutenant in the Dental Corps during World War I,
and a civic leader.[68] In referring to him, Slowe was acknowledging a devastating reality—the limits to her influence as a woman when dealing with a
sexist man, as well as the awareness that all her efforts and excellence were
being dismissed on the basis of her gender. She had spent her whole career encouraging young Black women to embrace their potential and claim
their right to be seen as modern subjects with wide horizons. The reality,
however, was that their aspirations—as well as her own—could be de-
limited and cast aside by the prerogative men exercised, even in the wom-
en's own communities. As Slowe rightly and painfully recognized, at her
alma mater and in the eyes of its first Black man president, "It means nothing to him that I am one of the few trained and experienced Deans in the
country."[69]

For the remainder of the summer, Johnson refused to identify an alternative residence to the shanty abutting the university dump. Having
fought this decision since April, just before the start of the 1933–34 school
year, Slowe attempted to resolve the matter by stating her intent to move
into one of the three dormitories.[70] However, she never relocated to university housing. A memo in her file suggests that what staved off the move
were letters of support sent to the Howard president and several board
members by Daniel Calhoun Roper, the secretary of commerce, and Carter Glass, a U.S. senator from Virginia.[71] Burrill's own handwritten annotation contends that "it was only after this political influence was secured
that Dean Slowe was given a partial rest from persecution."[72] This intercession provided what Slowe alone could not: the authority of more powerful actors, white politicians.[73]

Although Slowe remained in her private home off campus for the remainder of her career, tensions with Johnson and the board about her
housing situation continued into the 1933–34 academic year. Women students kept abreast of the pressure placed on Slowe and maintained their
vocal objection to the housing order. After the board denied two requests
by alumnae to meet with the trustees, Howard undergraduates staged a
public protest during the fall board meeting and collected student names in
support of their petition.[74] The *Baltimore Afro-American* reported on November 4, 1933: "A placard placed in the main building prior to the meeting of the board bore 'Girls, do you sanction the discrimination shown

99

between the dean of men and the dean of women? If you don't, please register today at 12 o'clock.'" Some men students stood in solidarity with the women against the trustees' refusal to grant them an audience.[75] Again, this action garnered much student support: the women collected more than 250 signatures, which were attached to a letter sent to Johnson as well as the board.

The *Baltimore Afro-American* reprinted the Howard women students' letter of concern in an article about the upcoming Twelfth Annual Women's Dinner. Identifying Slowe's residence as "the one home among those of the university officials that was always open to us," students framed the threat of forcing the dean to reside on campus as "destroy[ing] our only habitual retreat from the campus."[76] In this public and published resistance to the board and the Johnson administration, the Women's League—the official sponsor of the Women's Dinner—showed itself to be a political body and a forum for representing women's needs to masculinist constituencies and powers. At the actual dinner Slowe's remarks focused on what she termed "the crisis in higher education of women," suggesting a commentary relevant to the situation she and the women students knew well.[77]

Slowe's remuneration was another source of institutional devaluation. By the fall of 1933, when she was in her twelfth year of service, she had received a salary increase of only $300. All this had occurred during the Durkee administration, and it left her compensation within the Johnson years markedly below that of her men colleagues. Furthermore, it was $500 less than the salaried position of a junior high school principal that she had left to return to her alma mater eleven years earlier. In an unaddressed "Memorandum on the Department of the Dean of Women" dated October 9, 1933, Slowe recounted the terms of her original appointment, her purview as dean of women, and the disparagement she had experienced at Johnson's hands. In capital letters, she named the source of her frustration: "WOMEN'S PROGRAM HANDICAPPED SINCE THE ADMINISTRATION OF PRESIDENT JOHNSON." Furthermore, she revealed that her budget to cover programming for more than five hundred women students was a paltry $205.62 (equivalent to $4,178 today), from which she was also expected to cover her office needs.[78] In a later report Slowe estimated that this amount was just one-third of what she actually needed to promote intellectual and social activities for Howard women.[79] Nevertheless, Slowe pressed Johnson for a salary adjustment commensurate with her training and responsibilities. Even as late as August 1937, after yet another denial of a raise, she argued that hers was "an exceptional" case and insisted that Johnson take up the matter in March 1938 at the annual budget meeting of the board of trustees.[80]

The Death of a Daughter of Howard

Slowe never began the 1937–38 academic year. A bout of pneumonia in early August left her bedridden.[81] In those summer and fall months Slowe received a few letters from peers that referenced her "nervous exhaustion" and a state of cumulative debilitation.[82] However, the intensity of the professional attacks she had experienced for a decade appears to have been largely the cause. In a July 1937 letter to her former assistant Joanna Houston, Slowe lamented the departure of her former high school teacher and Howard University colleague, Dwight O. W. Holmes, for the presidency of Morgan State College. Slowe poignantly described the demoralization she was experiencing: "I regret very much to see him leave his Alma Mater, but I don't blame him in the least for making the decision to leave. It ought to be very refreshing to him to get into a different atmosphere and to work in a place where there is some consideration for human beings."[83]

The Black press kept its readers abreast of Slowe's rapidly failing condition. The September 18, 1937, edition of the *Baltimore Afro-American* reported that she was "critically ill" with pleurisy and noted that her relatives had already been "called to her bedside."[84] Two weeks later readers learned that Slowe had slipped into a coma at home.[85] Given the gravity of Slowe's decline, President Johnson was within his rights to name an interim dean of women as the new academic year approached. However, to the outrage of Burrill, as well as Slowe's closest friends and advocates, his humiliation of Slowe continued during her final weeks. In late September Johnson presented her, by way of her secretary, with what the *Alumni Journal* mordantly termed "the deathbed ultimatum": Slowe could either report to work or identify a replacement. Burrill refused to answer the demand, and the Howard administration replaced Slowe with her assistant, Alida Banks.[86]

The fifty-four-year-old Slowe died of kidney failure in her home at 11:05 p.m. on Thursday, October 21, 1937.[87] Her friends and supporters charged Johnson with "hate, ill-will and malice" toward her and consid-

ered her a "martyred example of [the] persecution, vindictiveness and ter-
rorism which rides wild and unchecked on Howard's campus."[88] Rallying
together, they banned him and other Howard administrators and trustees
from any official or symbolic role in her funeral services, which were held
in Rankin Memorial Chapel on the Howard campus at 1:00 p.m. on Mon-
day, October 25, 1937.[89]

Johnson's handwritten letter of condolence to Slowe's last surviving sib-
ling, her sister Nellie Hawkes, thanked her for a copy of the memorial service program and enclosed a few telegrams "expressing high esteem for
Dean Slowe and sympathy with the University in her loss." As Mary Burrill made clear in her own handwritten annotation on Johnson's letter, he
was focused on the logistics of the funeral and "neither . . . mentions the
great contributions that Lucy Slowe made to the University nor pays personal tribute to her outstanding worth."[90] It was a final snub to Burrill that
Johnson never offered his sympathies to her directly.

Banks, the interim dean of women, ushered in dramatic changes that
Howard women deemed unacceptable. In the first issue of the 1937–38 academic year, a *Hilltop* article referred to the three new staffers for the dormitories as matrons. Although these women were graduates of liberal arts
colleges, the use of the anachronistic term suggested a regressive approach
to the undergraduate women's dorm lives.[91] In a subsequent issue of the
newspaper, an editorial bearing the impertinent headline "Puh-lease, Miss
Banks" described Slowe's replacement as "the high-handed 'Hitler' of the
women's dormitory." It also accused her of falling in line with a majority of
campus administrators who "seem to be engaged in a contest to determine
the one official who can handle the students in the roughest manner."[92]
The headline on a second editorial in this issue asked rhetorically, "Whose
Dorms Are They?" in reference to a new practice of allowing faculty to live
in the women's residences, displacing women students in the process.

Undergraduate women's concerns about Slowe's successor contrasted
greatly with the *Hilltop*'s references to Slowe in the early fall. Notice of
her death was met with students' "deepest aggrievement" at the loss of "a
scholar and a friend." An editorial further described Slowe's distinguish-
ing qualities as "loyalty and devotion to duty with a deep-seated sympathy, so necessary to one in her office" and highlighted her effectiveness as
"a counsellor of students" who was equipped with "an innate ability" for
her work.[93] Slowe's obituary in the *Hilltop* remembered the dean as a be-

loved "Guide of University Women," and the editorial page of the November 10, 1937, issue included a somber pen-and-ink drawing of Slowe's closed office door beneath excerpts from Alfred, Lord Tennyson's elegy "Crossing the Bar."[94]

In a final editorial about Slowe, the *Baltimore Afro-American's* special correspondent described her as a martyr and "a victim to administrative vindictiveness" for her challenges to the gender order at Howard: "Whatever she wanted for the development of the women was very certain to meet with administrative opposition." He also praised her personal qualities: "She was no henchwoman. . . . She was a true woman, with a conscience that served as her daily companion. . . . Her life might have been prolonged if she had surrendered, but she fought as a real woman. She died as a real woman."[95] The reporter deemed valiant Slowe's New Negro Woman battle against Howard's patriarchal culture.

REMEMBERING DEAN LUCY DIGGS SLOWE

No one else can be Lucy Slowe in duplicate and there is no need to have another.
But the world is sorely in need of many to live as she has lived and to accomplish what
she has accomplished. There is still hard work to do and heavy loads to fill.... She
gave the last full measure of devotion that girls, all girls, might live more abundantly.

—Dr. Dwight O. W. Holmes, eulogy for Lucy Diggs Slowe, October 25, 1937

In the months after Slowe's funeral, Mary Burrill undertook an extensive
effort to expose Howard University's persecution of the dean and the du-
plicity of its administration. She ordered bound copies of Slowe's eulogy,
sent these to the trustees as well as to Slowe's professional colleagues, and
used the Black press—all to lay bare the harassment and hostility to which
the dean had been subjected for more than a decade. In Burrill's reply to
the condolence letter she received from the current board president, she
reminded him and the other trustees that few of their tributes "had found
expression in deeds before [Slowe's] passing." She confronted them with
their hypocrisy: "Howard University had in its midst in the person of Lucy
D. Slowe a great woman but its President and Board of Trustees could not
see it."[1]

Slowe's friend and colleague, Kelly Miller, the former Howard dean of
arts and sciences, also turned to the Black press to express his admiration
for Slowe's work. Significantly, he drew attention to the oppositional environment in which she labored, writing, "The Deanship of Women is perhaps the most important, as it is the most difficult and delicate position,
on any co-educational faculty. When Dean Slowe assumed her function

at Howard University she was given a skiff to sail an untried sea without chart or compass. She at once entered upon her task with the determination to solve this new problem in education." Miller's metaphor of a small boat traversing turbulent seas captured the unprecedented nature of Slowe's efforts as well as the combative context—"the masculine life of the University"—in which she undertook her advocacy of Black collegiate womanhood.[2] His powerful analogy also spoke to the tenacity of her purpose: the skiff moved across an expanse it was neither designed nor expected to navigate with success.

Miller's evocative words notwithstanding, it is important to note that the "untried sea[s]" that Slowe negotiated at Howard, as well as within the dean of women profession, were decidedly human made. The failure of some of her professional New Women colleagues to recognize her achievements and expertise and her disparagement by the patriarchal New Negro power structure at Howard University are sobering reminders that both groups were more invested in seeing Black women accommodate themselves to racism and sexism than in Slowe's New Negro Woman sense of intrinsic value. I read her early death as a tragic reminder of the price extracted from too many Black women who have dared to envision and work toward an inclusive world.

Howard alumnae, sorors, faculty, and friends expressed their shock and grief at Slowe's death in hundreds of telegrams and cards sent to Howard University and Mary Burrill. They also spoke to the breadth of the dean's influence. Ella Murphy, a Howard graduate, described to Burrill how Slowe uniquely "had the welfare of all women students at Howard at heart."[3] The sorority Slowe helped found, AKA, asserted that she "gave more than she received," and likened her forging of new spaces and possibilities for Black college women to gardening: "Where thorns and thistles once grew, she planted flowers."[4] The alumna Brenda Francke highlighted Slowe's "dynamic spirit," which was evident in her life and achievements.[5] From their many years of close association, Hilda Davis insisted that her mentor's work required both "vision and courage . . . to raise the status of the dean of women in Negro colleges to one of dignity and leadership."[6] Detroit-area AKA sorors characterized Slowe as a woman "filled with a keen insight into the social needs of a changing world." And because she "gave her life to building leaders with social vision," they considered the dean's death "a challenge to the womanhood of America."[7] Verna Dozier,

Lucy Diggs Slowe Memorial Stained Glass Window
in Rankin Chapel, Howard University.
Courtesy of Amber N. Wiley.

an alumna, concluded that "[Slowe] was fighting a great fight against ignorance, prejudice, bigotry," which were problems in society as well as in the hierarchical and exclusive contexts of higher education, including their own alma mater.[8]

Other letter writers spoke of their solidarity with the dean. In her condolences the chair of the 1931 Women's Dinner, Ketura Whitehurst, both lamented Slowe's "immeasurable loss" to future college women and emphasized how acutely Howard women identified with the dean. Although Slowe had been singled out for "unjust opposition and criticism," Whitehurst, class of 1932, vowed that "hundreds of us now" would take Slowe's place and embody "a spirit as militant and unconquerable." The alumna did not regard this conviction as an exaggeration, asserting, "I am sure I'm not alone in this opinion."[9] In a similar vein Marion Thompson Wright ('27) referred to Slowe enduringly as "my Dean" and herself as ever one of "her girls."[10]

Additional efforts to commemorate Slowe and her work continued for several years. The College Alumnae Club (CAC) of Washington, D.C., a group of Black women who were liberal arts graduates, worked with Mary Burrill to collect a representative sample of Slowe's writings, as well as tributes to the late dean. In January 1939 the CAC dedicated a memorial edition of its journal to Slowe's career and influence.[11] Howard students and alumnae also pursued institutional acknowledgment of the dean and her work. Pooling resources, they commissioned a stained-glass window for the Rankin Chapel of Howard University. Installed in November 1943, the window includes the inscription "Lucy Diggs Slowe, Pioneer, Friend, and Leader of Young Women."[12] These words complement the epitaph on her headstone, which reads, "Leader of Young Womanhood, Friend to All Humanity." Significantly, both tributes highlighted Slowe's commitment to Black college women. As a whole, these remembrances commemorated Slowe as both an educator and a beacon of Black women's possibility.

Because Slowe died just two weeks before what would have been the Sixteenth Annual Women's Dinner, Howard women held a tribute service in lieu of the celebratory gathering. They resolved, however, that the tradition would resume the next year in honor of Dean Slowe. Howard women not only organized the dinner in 1938 but sustained the intergenerational women's tradition at the university for almost half a century, until 1967.

At the Women's Dinner in November 1955, five hundred alumnae, students, and guests gathered for what had become a weekend celebration.[13] They paid homage to Slowe, her ideal of the New Howard Woman, and the institutional landscape she had reshaped for their benefit. Eighteen years after the dean's death, Vashti Turley Murphy, a Howard alumna, educator, and cofounder of Delta Sigma Theta, offered a poignant reflection on the historical necessity for Slowe's work: "Howard [University], Lucy Slowe found, was still an educational jungle, in the sense that it accepted women on the faculty grudgingly; that it paid them lower salaries than men; and that it considered its dean of women as dormitory preceptress or a house mother with a college education. . . . It was Lucy Slowe's task to bring to this university the conception of the Howard coed, who studies and gets her work, because that is what she is here for mainly."[14]

These women actively recalled the resistance Slowe faced on a campus "inhabited mainly by men not altogether convinced, that women were designed to do their equal share in the world's work."[15] Although Slowe encountered an institution overgrown with nineteenth-century attitudes toward Black women, through the founding of affirming traditions as well as structures, she cultivated a new "pleasure geography" for Howard women.[16] Like a diligent gardener, Slowe tended to their overlooked needs, sought to eliminate barriers to their growth, defended them against attacks on their worth, and nurtured their positive development in line with the self-affirming ethos of New Negro Womanhood and its rejection of racialized sexism and sexist racism.

When the gathering was in its fourth decade, an alumna stressed its ongoing significance: "Because Lucy Slowe set up that ideal [of Black womanhood] on this campus and persuaded the students to follow after it, tonight we have this dinner."[17] And almost two decades after her death, Howard women still were carrying her spirit forward—not only through the dinner but in the object of a cup presented to "the Howard senior, who approximates nearest the Lucy Slowe ideals of scholarship, character, culture, refinement, and high public service to the student body." The 1955 recipient sat on the student council as the senior class representative, served as a senior mentor and second vice president of the Women's League, and cochaired the Dean of Women's Committee.[18] She exemplified the leader-

Howard student Celestine Raven was the inaugural recipient of the Lucy Diggs Slowe Award in 1938.
Courtesy of Scurlock Studio Records, Archives Center,
National Museum of American History, Smithsonian Institution.

ship that Slowe had empowered Howard women to cultivate in their extra-curricular campus lives. The Howard women assembled in Slowe's honor still knew and respected the work the dean had undertaken to create insti-tutional space for them to "live more abundantly."

"I refuse to believe I am the first person to do this work." Ruth Nicole Brown, a scholar of Black girlhood studies, uttered these words to me at the 2017 National Women's Studies Association meeting as I shared with her the outlines of my project about Dean Slowe. What I find powerful about Brown's response is that she presumes her indebtedness to earlier scholar-activists—both known and yet to be found—who similarly rejected defi-cit framings of Black girl-woman subjectivities. Although separated by a century, Brown and Slowe share a conviction about the inherent value of young Black women in a dynamic stage of developing their minds, val-

Photo of Dean Slowe in her garden, 1932.
Courtesy of the Moorland-Spingarn Research Center,
Howard University Archives, Howard University, Washington, D.C.

ues, capacities, and sense of community. As such, both uphold New Negro Women ideals and support what we today call Black girl magic.[19]

A pioneer many times over, Dean Lucy Diggs Slowe was a higher education administrator and an innovator who led with an unyielding belief in young Black women as fully human beings. As such, she is a major feminist foremother in Howard's institutional history. From her own grounding in New Negro Womanhood, Slowe brought proud visibility to young Black women and their qualities as she knew them. Her personal example and ongoing championing of "my girls" outside "the double bind of white supremacy and respectability" allowed them to view themselves not as victims or subordinates but as equals, leaders, and necessary members of the many communities to which they belonged.[20]

The New Howard Woman embodied what Slowe saw as the essential qualities of "vision and imagination that enlarge our purposes and that keep us progressing all the time."[21] As a result, this Black feminist figure took up space, stated her truths, and stood alongside—and not behind—her peers from other race-gender groups. Black women living more abundantly operated not in the shadows of white people or Black men but in the light of their own selves and possibilities. Thus, instead of allowing their psyches to be populated with negative external perceptions and devaluations, Slowe cultivated collective, affirming spaces for Black college women to determine their own value and outlooks. The New Howard Woman, as a New Negro Woman, saw herself as nothing less than a full and deserving citizen of a new century. And for its attention to Black women's self-definition, its creation of joyous and supportive environments, and its challenges to structures of exclusion, Slowe's audacious philosophy of living more abundantly remains a relevant and necessary labor—in higher education as well as society at large.

Lucy Diggs Slowe, loyal daughter of Howard University, molder of finer womanhood, inspirer of youth, dreamer and worker for a better day for Negro women, may your memory continue to be an inspiration.[22]

NOTES

Preface

1. Warren, "Black Behind the Black and Gold."
2. Heldke, "A DuBoisian Proposal," 224.

Introduction

The epigraph is drawn from Hilda A. Davis, "Howard Women's Dinner Speech," November 7, 1941, box 90-1, folder 9, Lucy Diggs Slowe (LDS) Papers.

1. "First Annual Howard Women's Dinner," 88.

2. Bertha McNeill (1887–1979) was a Howard University alumna, Slowe's roommate, and an Alpha Kappa Alpha sister. From 1932 into the late 1950s, she served as chair of the Interracial Committee of the Women's International League for Peace and Freedom. See Blackwell-Johnson, "African American Activists," 472; Miller and Pruitt-Logan, *Faithful to the Task at Hand*, 284; Facebook post by the Swarthmore College Peace Collection, February 22, 2017, https://www.facebook.com/SwarthmoreCollegePeaceCollection/posts/1296676630379270; "First Annual Howard Women's Dinner," 88.

3. The last mention I found of the Women's Dinner was in 1967, the year of the forty-fifth annual banquet. The Association of Women Students organized that dinner, which concluded an entire Women's Week. "Women's Week Takes International Flavor," *Hilltop*, November 10, 1967.

4. References to Slowe's birth year are inconsistent. The Finding Aid at Howard lists the year as 1883 (https://dh.howard.edu/cgi/viewcontent.cgi?article=1174&context=finaid_manu), as does an affidavit after her death. Miller and Pruitt-Logan, *Faithful to the Task at Hand*, 352n5. Her eulogy includes no birth year, but a death notice in *Washington, D.C.'s Evening Star* ("Deaths Reported," October 25, 1937), Alpha Kappa Alpha's website (https://aka1908.com/about/founders), and her Wikipedia entry (https://en.wikipedia.org

/wiki/Lucy_Diggs_Slowe) reference 1885. Slowe herself did not include a birth year in her autobiographical statements. I use 1883 as Slowe's birth year.

5. "In Memoriam: Eulogy by Dwight O. W. Holmes," October 25, 1937, box 90-1, folder 1, LDS Papers.

6. "A Woman Without a Country," box 90-6, folder 151, LDS Papers.

7. Cuthbert, "Letter of Condolences," 70–71.

8. "The Business of Being a Dean of Women," undated but ca. 1932, box 90-6, folder 119, LDS Papers.

9. Higginbotham, *Righteous Discontent*; Washington, "Democracy and Education."

10. Reid-Brinkley, "Essence of Res(ex)pectability."

11. See, for example, Evans, *Black Women in the Ivory Tower*; Guy-Sheftall, *Daughters of Sorrow*; Harley, "Beyond the Classroom"; Neverdon-Morton, "Self-Help Programs as Educative Activities"; Perkins, "Role of Education"; Shaw, *What a Woman Ought to Be and Do.*

12. Crocco and Waite, "Education and Marginality," 73.

13. Hine, "Rape and the Inner Lives of Black Women."

14. Evans, *Black Women in the Ivory Tower*, 64; Brittney C. Cooper, *Beyond Respectability*, 21.

15. Brittney C. Cooper, *Beyond Respectability*, 5; Curwood, *Stormy Weather*; Lindsey, *Colored No More.*

16. Brittney C. Cooper, *Beyond Respectability*, 5; Chatelain, *South Side Girls*; Simmons, *Crescent City Girls*; Harley, "Nannie Helen Burroughs."

17. Lindsey, "Climbing the Hilltop."

18. During Stowe's term in office, the weekly *Afro-American*, based in Baltimore, covered her avidly, as did the *Evening Star*, the daily then considered the paper of record in Washington, D.C. The *Afro-American* also published a Washington, D.C., edition after April 1931, as well as sporadic regional and national editions after December 1934, and these editions usually would have carried the *Afro*'s stories about her.

19. See, for example, Karen Anderson, "Brickbats and Roses"; Bell-Scott, "'To Keep My Self-Respect'"; Bell-Scott, "Business of Being a Dean of Women"; Lindsey, *Colored No More* and "Climbing the Hilltop"; Perkins, "Lucy Diggs Slowe"; and Rasheed, "Lucy Diggs Slowe" and *Lucy Diggs Slowe.*

20. Marion Thompson Wright was a Howard alumna who entered the university in Slowe's second year as dean. In January 1927 Wright served as president of the Women's League. In 1961 Wright, the first African American historian to earn a doctoral degree from Columbia University, received a grant from the *Evening Star* to write Slowe's biography. However, Wright died a year later, before the manuscript was finished. Miller and Pruitt-Logan, *Faithful to the Task at Hand*, 109, 141; Daniel, "A Tribute to Marion Thompson Wright," 310. Wright's work was foundational to the 2012 biography of Slowe by Miller and Pruitt-Logan, *Faithful to the Task at Hand.*

21. Haynes et al., "Toward an Understanding of Intersectionality Methodology," 753. See also Cole and Guy-Sheftall, *Gender Talk*; Njoku, Butler, and Beatty, "Reimagining the Historically Black College and University."

22. Lindsey, *Colored No More.*

23. Brittney C. Cooper, *Beyond Respectability*, 99. See also Fleming, "Black Women"; Kennedy, "HBCU Experience"; and Haynes et al., "Toward an Understanding of Intersectionality Methodology."

24. Jones and Shorter-Gooden, *Shifting*, 39.

25. Brittney C. Cooper, *Beyond Respectability*, 94.

26. Robinson and Ward, "A Belief in Self," 87.

Chapter 1. Refusing Respectabilities

1. Smith, *Reparation and Reconciliation*, 190.

2. Simmons, "'To Lay Aside all Morals,'" 434, 431. See also Monica Anderson, "A Look at Historically Black Colleges"; Tice, *Queens of Academe.*

3. Lowe, *Looking Good*, 41.

4. Bertaux and Anderson, "An Emerging Tradition of Educational Achievement," 17, 18.

5. McDaniel et al., "Black Gender Gap in Educational Attainment"; Shaw, *What a Woman Ought to Be and Do.*

6. Amott and Matthaei, *Race, Gender, and Work*, 158, 125.

7. Crocco and Waite, "Education and Marginality," 75; Shaw, *What a Woman Ought to Be and Do*; Perkins, "Impact of the 'Cult of True Womanhood.'"

8. Noble, "Higher Education of Black Women," 96. See also Harley, "Beyond the Classroom."

9. Graham, "Women in Academe"; Nidiffer, "Crumbs from the Boy's Table."

10. Newcomer, *A Century of Higher Education*, 37.

11. Ibid., 46.

12. Lowe, *Looking Good*; Palmieri, *In Adamless Eden*; Turk, *Bound by a Mighty Vow.*

13. Palmieri, *In Adamless Eden*, 4.

14. Palmieri, "Symmetrical Womanhood."

15. Palmer, "A Review of the Higher Education of Women," 33, 29.

16. Talbot, *Education of Women*, viii.

17. Porter, "Physical Hindrances to Teaching Girls," 48.

18. Smith-Rosenberg, *Disorderly Conduct*, 253.

19. MacDonald, "American Social Settlements," 5.

20. See, for example, Addams, *Newer Ideals of Peace.*

21. Perkins, "African American Female Elite"; Smith, *Reparation and Reconciliation*, 6.

22. Perkins, "African American Female Elite," 722.

23. Ibid., 734.

24. Patterson, *Beyond the Gibson Girl.*

25. Bashaw, *Stalwart Women.*

26. Lowe, *Looking Good*; Turk, *Bound by a Mighty Vow.*

27. Smith-Rosenberg, *Disorderly Conduct*, 203.

28. Jones, *A Personnel Study of Women Deans*, 12.

29. Nidiffer, "Advocates on Campus," 152.

30. Bashaw, *Stalwart Women*, 2.

31. Phillips, Kerr, and Wells, "History of the National Association of Deans of Women," 228–29.

32. Palmieri, *In Adamless Eden*.

33. Bordin, *Alice Freeman Palmer*, 240.

34. Rosenberry, *Dean of Women*, 14.

35. Jones, *A Personnel Study of Women Deans*; Schwartz, "Reconceptualizing the Leadership Roles of Women."

36. Bashaw, *Stalwart Women*, ix.

37. Horowitz, *Campus Life*, 194; Zimmerman, "Daughters of Main Street," 158.

38. Haidarali, "New Howard Woman Goes to Campus," 23; Lowe, *Looking Good*.

39. Duffy, "How Women Impacted the Historical Development," 244.

40. Amos, "Unsocial Aspects of the Social Curriculum," 8.

41. Ibid., 12.

42. Slowe, "Place of the Dean of Women on the College Campus," 54.

43. Slowe, "Dean of Women," 112.

44. Rosenberry, *Dean of Women*, 159.

45. Bashaw, "Reassessment and Redefinition," 177.

46. Rosenberry, *Dean of Women*, 225–26.

47. Ibid., 223, 122.

48. Pierce, *Deans and Advisers of Women and Girls*, 1.

49. Sturtevant, "Qualifications and Preparation of Deans of Women," 119–20.

50. Ibid., 120.

51. "Unusually Costumed Partners Appear at Co-ed Prom," *Pitt News*, October 11, 1932.

52. Such celebrated cross-dressing among women students was not limited to the University of Pittsburgh. A 1930 article in the *Pittsburgh Press* described the second annual, sorority-sponsored, "manless" co-ed prom at nearby Waynesburg College. "Waynesburg Has Manless Dance," *Pittsburgh Press*, February 16, 1930.

53. In Slowe's 1936 address to the meeting of the Deans and Advisors in Colored Schools at Wilberforce University, she references an essay by H. L. Mencken, "Lady Cops in Cap and Gown," which depicted deans of women as "polic[ing] the campus." Slowe, "Place of the Dean of Women on the College Campus."

54. Pierce, *Deans and Advisers of Women and Girls*, 1; Slowe, "Higher Education of Negro Women," 352.

55. Schwartz, "Reconceptualizing the Leadership Roles of Women."

56. Schwartz, *Deans of Men and the Shaping of Modern Culture*.

57. Gaston-Gayles et al., "From Disciplinarian to Change Agent."

58. Whitney, "Women Student Personnel Administrators," 8.

59. Schmitt, "Deans of Women in U.S. Higher Education," 55. See also Hevel, "Toward a History of Student Affairs," 848.

60. Slowe, "Dean of Women in a Modern University," 9.

61. Lindsey, *Colored No More.*
62. Dotson, "Theorizing Jane Crow," 424.
63. Evans, *Black Women in the Ivory Tower*, 72.
64. Lindsey, *Colored No More*; Brittney C. Cooper, *Beyond Respectability.*
65. Lindsey, *Colored No More*, 2.
66. Perkins, "African American Female Elite."
67. Anna Julia Cooper, "Intellectual Progress of the Colored Women," 204–205.
68. Ibid., 205, 204.
69. Lindsey, *Colored No More*, 8.
70. Williams, "Intellectual Progress of the Colored Women," 24, 26.
71. Curwood, "A Fresh Look," 326.
72. Harper, "Woman's Political Future," 433–34.
73. Williams, "Intellectual Progress of the Colored Women," 20.
74. Anna Julia Cooper, "Status of Woman in America," 112–13.
75. Brown, "College Woman Accepts the Challenge," 5–6.
76. Melancon, *Unbought and Unbossed*, 49.
77. Williams, "Colored Girl," 63.
78. Ibid., 65, 64, 65, 63, 64.
79. Anna Julia Cooper, "Higher Education of Women," 86, 80, 87.
80. Nazera Wright, *Black Girlhood in the Nineteenth Century*, 3, 39.
81. Chatelain, *South Side Girls.*
82. "Vocational Guidance," 76.
83. Chatelain, *South Side Girls*, 109.
84. McDougald, "Task of Negro Womanhood," 74.
85. "New Negro Woman," 757.
86. Lindsey, *Colored No More*; McCluskey, "'We Specialize in the Wholly Impossible.'"
87. Robinson, "M Street High School, 1891–1916," 122–23.
88. Johnson, "Gender and Race," 75.
89. Ibid., 76; Lindsey, "Configuring Modernities," 1; Waite, "DuBois and the Invisible Talented Tenth."
90. Johnson, "'In Service for the Common Good,'" 50.
91. Taylor, "'Womanhood Glorified,'" 395.
92. Ibid., 398.
93. Harley, "Nannie Helen Burroughs," 65; McCluskey, "'We Specialize in the Wholly Impossible,'" 420.
94. Taylor, "'Womanhood Glorified,'" 400.
95. Bair, "Educating Black Girls."
96. Taylor, "'Womanhood Glorified,'" 394.
97. Ibid., 395.
98. McCluskey, "'We Specialize in the Wholly Impossible,'" 423.
99. Slowe's siblings included two brothers (William Myers and John A.) and two sisters (Nellie Slowe Hawkes and Charlotte E. Slowe). According to their obituaries, Wil-

liam Slowe was a Philadelphia dentist who died in 1923. Her brother John, a restaurant owner and Pullman porter, died in August 1931. Her sister, Charlotte Slowe, was a social science high school teacher and principal in Delaware; she died in February 1937, just eight months before the dean's death. Slowe was survived by one sister, Nellie Slowe Hawkes of Philadelphia.

100. "Summer School," May 23, 1935, box 90-1, folder 1, LDS Papers. See also "Meet Dean Slowe," *Hilltop*, December 11, 1930.

101. Karen Anderson, "From 'Brickbats and Roses,'" 135.

102. Coralie Franklin Cook, "Lucy D. Slowe—Student," n.d., box 90-1, folder 9, LDS Papers.

103. "College of Arts and Sciences, Graduating Class of 1908," lists Slowe as one of eight or nine women graduates in the class. The text reads, "The largest class in the history of this college was graduated last spring. The distribution of these seventeen graduates among the different callings and professions is indicative of the wide range of opportunity open to college men." Although the article refers to seventeen graduates of the College of Arts and Sciences in 1908, it lists only sixteen names—eight women and eight men. A listing of graduates in the city's major daily includes nineteen names from the liberal arts undergraduate program. "Commencement Exercises," *Evening Star* (Washington, D.C.), May 27, 1908.

104. "Paragraphic News," *Bee* (Washington, D.C.), June 27, 1908.

105. "Miss Slowe Now 'Lady Principal,'" *Baltimore Afro-American*, October 4, 1918. Teachers College, Columbia University, was the site of the first graduate program for the profession of deans of women, and Slowe took courses toward her doctorate in the field. Clarence Linton to Slowe, July 29, 1930, box 90-3, folder 77, LDS Papers. In fall 1922 she became the first African American member of the National Association of Deans of Women.

106. Lounsbury, "Deferred but Not Deterred"; "Public Schools Sorry to Lose Lucy Slowe," *Baltimore Afro-American*, June 22, 1922.

107. Lounsbury, "Deferred but Not Deterred," 35.

108. "Shaw Junior High School," *Evening Star*, June 18, 1922.

109. Miller and Pruitt-Logan, *Faithful to the Task at Hand*, 54.

110. "Columbia University Extension Center at Shaw Junior High to Continue," *Evening Star*, September 30, 1922. See also "Introductory Remarks by Esther A. B. Popel from Proceedings of the Conference of College Women called by The College Alumnae Club," box 90-6, folder 145, LDS Papers; "Shaw High Faculty Helps Plan Course," *Washington Post*, Sunday, May 13, 1923; and Marion Thompson Wright, "Slowe, Lucy Diggs."

111. "Shaw Junior High School," *Evening Star*, February 26, 1922. See also "Miss Slowe Honored," *Evening Star*, June 6, 1922; and "Colored Teachers Form Columbian Association," *Evening Star*, February 11, 1922.

112. "Shaw Junior High School," *Evening Star*, June 18, 1922.

113. "Miss Slowe for Women's Suffrage," *Baltimore Afro-American*, October 23, 1915.

114. "Honor Dean Slowe at Tennis Meeting," *Washington Afro-American*, August 27,

1938. See also "Grand Slam: History of Blacks in Tennis," *Black Enterprise*, September 1, 1994, https://www.thefreelibrary.com/Grand+Slam%3A+history+of+blacks+in+tennis .-a015752092.

115. Lindsey, *Colored No More*.

Chapter 2. We Are the New Howard Woman

1. Neale, "New Howard Woman," 49.

2. Ibid.

3. "Role of a Sorority," *Hilltop*, April 14, 1937.

4. Neale, "New Howard Woman," 49.

5. Logan, *Howard University*, 170. Slowe was the first full-time, trained dean of women at Howard University. Reflecting the gender attitudes of most coeducational institutions, two other women had served in more supervisory roles before Slowe. In the early 1900s Marie I. Hardwick was known as the "matron of Miner Hall," the women's dormitory before the erection of the Women's Campus. "Former Dean of Women Honored at H.U. Dinner," *Baltimore Afro-American*, November 17, 1945; "Miss Hardwick Dies in Georgia," *Baltimore Afro-American*, April 20, 1946. Slowe's immediate predecessor was an instructor of physical education, Helen Hale Tuck, who had been named Howard University's acting dean of women in June 1920 and served on a part-time basis until June 30, 1922. Logan, *Howard University*, 198–99.

6. "Dean of Women Talked to Men," 51–52.

7. Holmes, *Evolution of the Negro College*.

8. Smith, *Reparation and Reconciliation*, 81.

9. Lindsey, *Colored No More*, 20.

10. "First Annual Howard Women's Dinner," 90.

11. Ibid., 88.

12. Miller and Pruitt-Logan, *Faithful to the Task at Hand*, 102.

13. "First Annual Howard Women's Dinner," 88.

14. Ibid., 90.

15. "Howard Women Hold First Annual," 86.

16. Simmons, *Crescent City Girls*, 190.

17. "Annual Howard Women's Dinner," November 9, 1923, box 90-5, folder 111, LDS Papers; "Second Annual Women's Dinner," 148.

18. "Our Dean of Women," 79.

19. "300 Undergraduate Howard Women Sit Down at Annual Dinner," *Baltimore Afro-American*, November 15, 1930.

20. "Undergraduate Life," 86.

21. "Press Service, Howard University. Annual Women's Dinner at Howard Now an Important University Event," n.d. but ca. November 1924, box 90-10, folder 192, LDS Papers.

22. "Third Annual Women's Dinner Huge Success," *Hilltop*, November 14, 1924.

23. "Women's Dinner Speaker Stresses Enormous Purchasing Power of Group; Urges Its Use," *Pittsburgh Courier*, November 17, 1934; "Women Hold 14th Dinner," *Hilltop*, November 13, 1935; "To Sing at H.U. Dinner," *Afro-American*, October 24, 1936, final Washington, D.C., ed.

Mary McCleod Bethune, president of Bethune-Cookman College in Daytona Beach, Florida, and director of Negro affairs for the National Youth Association, spoke at the first dinner after the dean's death. "The Late Dean Slowe Honored Before 500 at Women's Dinner," *Hilltop*, November 21, 1938. Subsequent speakers included Dr. Mamie P. Clark, the Howard alumna who founded and served as director of New York City's Northside Center for Child Development. "College Women Hold First Week End Meet at Howard U," *Baltimore Afro-American*, November 6, 1954. Ruth B. Quarles, a member of the American Council on Education's Commission for Women in Higher Education, spoke at the 1955 dinner. "Final Arrangements Made for Annual H.U. Women's Weekend," *Afro-American*, November 5, 1955, national ed. Bruce was sister to Slowe's life partner, Mary Burrill. Rasheed, *Lucy Diggs Slowe*, 82N26.

24. "Women's Column: The Women's Dinner a Great Success," *Hilltop*, November 7, 1928; "Women's Activities," *Hilltop*, November 7, 1929.

25. "Women's Column."

26. "Women's Activities," *Hilltop*, November 7, 1929.

27. Ibid., November 13, 1930.

28. "Women's Leaguers Parade Attracts to Annual Dinner" and "Women Hold Annual Dinner Gala Event," *Hilltop*, November 10, 1933.

29. "Girls in Modern Life," *Hilltop*, November 7, 1924.

30. "First Annual Howard Women's Dinner," 89.

31. Ibid., 89–90.

32. "If Women May Speak," *Hilltop*, May 15, 1930.

33. "Women's Activities," *Hilltop*, October 15, 1931.

34. "300 Women Honor Dean at Dinner," *Hilltop*, November 10, 1932.

35. "Annual Congressional Appropriation of $500,000 Suggested," 295.

36. Tribute by Margaret Jean Grooms, "Lucy Diggs Slowe First Dean of Women of Howard University 1922–1937," n.d., box 90-1, folder 10, LDS Papers.

37. "Dean Slowe Honored," *Baltimore Afro-American*, November 14, 1931. See also program for Tenth Annual Howard Women's Dinner, November 6, 1931, box 90-5, folder III, LDS Papers.

38. "500 Dine at H.U. Women's 15th Dinner," *Baltimore Afro-American*, November 14, 1936.

39. "H.U. Women Hold 15th Annual Dinner," *Hilltop*, November 11, 1936.

40. "300 Undergraduate Howard Women Sit Down at Annual Dinner," *Baltimore Afro-American*, November 15, 1930.

41. "H.U. Women Hold 15th Annual."

42. Slowe to Johnson, and "Fifteenth Annual Report of the Dean of Women," June 30, 1937, box 90-5, folder 114, LDS Papers.

43. Slowe, "Colored Girl Enters College," 279. See also "Fifteenth Annual Report."

44. "Ten Women Made Senior Mentors for Frosh Students," *Hilltop*, September 25, 1933. See also "They Advise Freshman Girls," *Hilltop*, October 12, 1933; and "Howard Women Run Themselves in New Dorms," *Baltimore Afro-American*, August 20, 1932.

45. "The Mentors' Magna Cum Laude," *Hilltop*, October 19, 1936.

46. Hilda A. Davis, Howard Women's Dinner Speech, November 7, 1941, box 90-1, folder 9, LDS Papers.

47. Slowe annual report to Durkee, May 23, 1923.

48. Ibid. In an April 26, 1933, memo to the board of trustees in which Slowe contested their decision to cut her staff (laying off the women's physician, graduate dietician, and one of the dormitory directors), Slowe mentions three hundred women students were living off campus and her responsibility for "the welfare of over four hundred women." Slowe memo to board of trustees, April 26, 1933, box 90-5, folder 113, LDS Papers. In Slowe's fifteenth and final annual report in 1937, she mentions supervising the activities of "over 800" women students and notes that 195 students lived in the dormitories. She also identifies a budget of only $200 to support extracurricular activities for the women, who numbered 897 in the spring semester. In this report she presses for several additions to her staff—a full-time assistant dean of women, a second secretary, a return to 1931 salaries for the directors of two of the dormitories, and a tripling of her budget to $600. Slowe, "1937 Annual Report of the Dean of Women addressed to President Johnson, June 30, 1937," box 90-5, folder 114, LDS Papers.

49. "Annual Congressional Appropriation of $500,000 Suggested," 295.

50. "1,500 Attend Opening of New Dorms," *Hilltop*, December 10, 1931; "Howard U. Places Dormitory Stone," *Evening Star* (Washington, D.C.), June 5, 1931.

51. "1,500 Attend Opening of New Dorms"; "Howard Opens," *Evening Star*, October 4, 1931, pt. 1; "Howard Women Run Themselves." Slowe's staff included an assistant to the dean of women, Joanna Houston, and a director of residences, Elaine Tancil. Both women had trained at Teachers College and taught in the English department in addition to their work for Slowe. "Significant Achievement in the Department of the Dean of Women, Howard University," undated but ca. June 1932, box 90-5, folder 113, LDS Papers.

52. "Significant Achievement."

53. "Howard Women Run Themselves."

54. Heath, "Our Heritage Speaks," 15.

55. "Mentors' Magna Cum Laude."

56. "Dean Lucy D. Slowe," box 90-1, folder 1, LDS Papers. See also "Significant Achievement."

57. "Girls' Basketball," *Hilltop*, November 8, 1927.

58. "Co-Eds Establish W.A.A. to Promote Sports at Howard," *Hilltop*, December 10, 1931.

59. See "Intramurals Schedules for Women Arranged," *Hilltop*, November 10, 1932; "W.A.A. Appoints Women's Coaches," *Hilltop*, November 24, 1932; "W.A.A. Plans to Give Tap Dancing," *Hilltop*, October 12, 1933.

60. "Bustles and Laces from the Gay Nights of the Nineties," *Hilltop*, March 6, 1935; "Women Give Date," *Hilltop*, January 20, 1936; "Women to Give Costumer Ball February 5," *Hilltop*, January 27, 1937.

61. "Women Turn Tables at Valentine Party," *Hilltop*, February 21, 1936.

62. "Frivolity Day at Howard University: Campus Witnesses Gay Sights," *Hilltop*, May 15, 1930.

63. "Among the Many Interesting Adjuncts." See also "Outline of Duties of the Dean of Women," December 1925, box 90-2, folder 52, and Slowe annual report to J. Stanley Durkee, May 23, 1923, box 90-2, folder 52, both in LDS Papers.

64. "Co-Eds Display Abilities at Closed Party: Original Skits Presented," *Hilltop*, February 4, 1932.

65. "Women's Faculty Club Party Has Contests, Games," *Hilltop*, November 17, 1934.

66. "Women's Activities," *Hilltop*, November 7, 1929.

67. Ibid.

68. "Delta Sigma Theta Sorority House," 90.

69. Zena Martin, "Delta Sigma Theta—Leading Ladies in Red," *Books & Belonging* (blog), February 4, 2013, http://zmblackhistorymonth2013.blogspot.com/2013/02/delta-sigma-theta-leading-ladies-in-red_4.html.

70. Lindsey, "Configuring Modernities," 130; See also Michelle Bernard, "Despite the Tremendous Risk, African American Women Marched for Suffrage, Too," *Washington Post*, March 3, 2013, https://www.washingtonpost.com/blogs/she-the-people/wp/2013/03/03/despite-the-tremendous-risk-african-american-women-marched-for-suffrage-too/.

71. "Anne Arnold Hedgeman to Be Guest Speaker at Annual Women's Dinner at Howard Univ.," *New York Age*, November 8, 1941.

72. Slowe annual report to Durkee, May 23, 1923.

73. "Role of a Sorority."

74. "Howard Women Hold First Annual."

75. Slowe, "Future of the Association of College Women," 28.

76. Cromwell, "Proposed National Federation," 11.

77. Perkins, "Lucy Diggs Slowe," 89.

78. Davis and Bell-Scott, "Association of Deans of Women," 41. See also "Report of Ten Years' Work, By Committee on Standards, NACW," 1933, box 90-9, folder 190, LDS Papers.

79. During its twenty-five-year existence (1929–54), the NAWDACS carried different names. Perkins ("Lucy Diggs Slowe") refers to it as the National Association of Women's Deans and Advisers of Colored Schools. Hilda Davis, who succeeded Slowe in leading the group, termed it the Association of Deans of Women and Counselors of Girls in Negro Colleges and Schools. Brett et al., "A Symposium," 53. In their entry for the historical encyclopedia *Black Women in America*, Hilda Davis and Patricia Bell-Scott write about the Association of Deans of Women and Advisers to Girls in Negro Schools. In 1954 the organization Slowe founded joined with the National Association of Personnel Deans of Men at Negro Educational Institutions to become the National Association of Person-

nel Workers. Davis and Bell-Scott, "Association of Deans of Women," 49, 51. Today it is known as the National Association of Student Affairs Professionals.

80. Slowe, "The Education of Negro Women and Girls," address to Teachers College, March 11, 1931, box 90-6, folder 130, LDS Papers. An article in the *Baltimore Afro-American*, "Columbia Hears Dean Slowe of Howard," (March 21, 1931), states that the title of her talk was "The Education of Negro College Women for Social Responsibility."

81. Slowe, "Higher Education of Negro Women," 354.

82. Slowe, "Education of Negro Women and Girls."

83. Slowe, "Higher Education of Negro Women," 356, 357.

84. Ibid., 355, 358, 356.

85. Slowe, "Colored Girl Enters College," 277.

86. Slowe, "Higher Education of Negro Women," 355.

87. Slowe, "Education of Negro Women and Girls."

88. Slowe, "Higher Education of Negro Women," 354–55.

89. "Women Dined by Dean Slowe: Discuss Campus Inertia among Women Leaders," *Hilltop*, November 28, 1934.

90. Perkins, "Lucy Diggs Slowe," 97.

91. Slowe, "Education of Negro Women and Girls."

92. Evans, *Black Women in the Ivory Tower*, 68; Slowe, "Education of Negro Women and Girls."

93. Slowe, "Higher Education of Negro Women," 355.

94. Noble, *Negro Woman's College Education*, 26.

95. "Women's Annual Vocational Conference Close," *Hilltop*, April 30, 1930.

96. Slowe, "Colored Girl Enters College," 278.

97. "Women's Conferences at Howard University," *Baltimore Afro-American*, April 19, 1930, city ed.

98. "Women's Annual Vocational Conference Close," *Hilltop*, April 30, 1930.

99. Hilda Davis to Beatrice Walker, December 14, 1938, box 90-1, folder 2, LDS Papers.

100. "Outline of Duties of the Dean of Women."

101. "Course for Deans of Women," *Hilltop*, May 15, 1930; "Changes in H.U. Faculty," *Baltimore Afro-American*, October 6, 1928; "All Quiet on H.U. Front after Co-Ed Flare-Up," *Baltimore Afro-American*, December 17, 1938.

102. Slowe to Mabel Carney, Teachers College, December 21, 1933, box 90-2, folder 37, LDS Papers.

103. Slowe, "Education of Negro Women and Girls."

104. "Can Our Women Develop into Capable, Efficient Leaders?" *Norfolk (Va.) Journal and Guide*, March 28, 1931; Slowe, "Colored Girl Enters College," 278.

105. Valerie O'Mega Justiss to Miss Beatrice Walker, November 5, 1938, box 90-1, folder 3, LDS Papers.

106. Haidarali, "New Negro Woman Goes to Campus," 25. Although she recognizes Slowe's commitment to young women's self-determination, Haidarali highlights generational tensions regarding students' sexual freedom and leisure, and she characterizes

Slowe as still adhering to tenets of respectability. There are certainly accounts of women students who were expelled or temporarily dismissed for staying out past curfew (e.g., "Four Howard University Coeds Expelled," *Chicago Defender*, December 19, 1936; "To Reinstate Howard Girls," *Chicago Defender*, January 2, 1937). Hilda Davis also notes student "opposition and occasional hostility" in the early years of Slowe's tenure, as well as the dean's success within two or three years in gaining the respect and confidence of the majority ("Tribute to Dean Slowe," 72). However, as I explore in this chapter and chapter 4, I find much more evidence of student receptiveness to, and partnership with, Slowe about the ideal of the New Howard Woman, as it affirmed their personal development and social awareness.

107. Davis, "It Gives Me Great Pleasure," 72.

108. "Women Dined by Dean Slowe," *Hilltop*, November 28, 1934.

109. Slowe, "Business of Being a Dean of Women," box 90-6, folder 119, LDS Papers.

110. Haidarali, "New Negro Woman Goes to Campus," 18.

111. Combahee River Collective, "Combahee River Collective Statement."

Chapter 3. Race Work Is Women's Work

The first epigraph is drawn from Miller and Pruitt-Logan, *Faithful to the Task at Hand*, 336.

1. "60 Visiting Deans Praise H.U. Dorms," *Baltimore Afro-American*, March 5, 1932.

2. Bailey, "Locating Traitorous Identities."

3. Thyrsa W. Amos to Slowe, June 1, 1931, box 90-2, folder 23, LDS Papers.

4. Slowe, "Future of the Association of College Women," 28.

5. "Dean Slowe Speaks at National Association," 334.

6. Blitz, "Social Conditions Arising from Inter-Racial Contact," 75–76.

7. Ibid., 78.

8. Slowe to Anne Blitz regarding student housing, October 23, 1936, Dean of Women, box 1, folder 16, Negro, University of Minnesota Archives, http://acampusdivided.umn .edu/index.php/letter/lucy-slowe-letter-to-anne-blitz-regarding-student-housing/.

9. Sarah Atwood, Patrick Wilz, Rachel Hertzberg, and Rose Miron, "Segregated Student Housing and the Activists Who Defeated It," in the digital exhibit *A Campus Divided: Progressives, Anticommunists, Racism and Antisemitism at the University of Minnesota 1930–1942*, 2017, http://acampusdivided.umn.edu/index.php/essay/segregated -student-housing/.

10. Anne Blitz to Lucy Diggs Slowe, November 23, 1936, Dean of Women, box 1, folder 16, Negro, University of Minnesota Archives, reproduced in the digital exhibit *A Campus Divided*, http://acampusdivided.umn.edu/index.php/letter/anne-blitz-to-lucy-slowe -responding-to-query/.

11. Lucy Diggs Slowe to Anne Blitz, November 23, 1936, Dean of Women, box 1, folder 16, Negro, University of Minnesota Archives, reproduced in the digital exhibit *A Campus Divided*, http://acampusdivided.umn.edu/index.php/letter/lucy-diggs-slowe-reply-to-anne -blitz-regarding-students/.

12. Charlotte Crump, "This Free North," *Literary Review*, April 5, 1937, Dean of

Women, box 1, folder 16, Negro, University of Minnesota Archives, reproduced in the digital exhibit *A Campus Divided*, http://acampusdivided.umn.edu/index.php/text/this -free-north-in-university-literary-magazine/.

13. Ibid., 12.

14. Anne Blitz to Charlotte Crump, Dean of Women, box 1, folder 16, Negro, University of Minnesota Archives, reproduced in the digital exhibit *A Campus Divided*, http:// acampusdivided.umn.edu/index.php/letter/anne-blitz-letter-to-charlotte-crump-about-this -free-north/.

15. Lucy Jenkins Franklin to Slowe, November 7, 1930, box 90-3, folder 60, LDS Papers. Franklin was also the chair of the Urban University section of the NADW, to which Slowe belonged. See Thyrsa Amos to Slowe, May 10, 1929, box 90-2, folder 23, LDS Papers.

16. Slowe to Lucy Jenkins Franklin, dean of Boston University, November 12, 1930, box 90-3, folder 60, LDS Papers.

17. Ibid.

18. Ibid.

19. Hilda A. Davis (1905–2001) completed the dean of women graduate course at Boston University. She earned a master's degree in English Literature from Radcliffe and a doctoral degree in human development from the University of Chicago. Davis served as dean of women and professor of English at Shaw University and Talladega College.

20. Brett et al., "A Symposium," 53.

21. "60 Visiting Deans Praise H.U. Dorms," *Baltimore Afro-American*, March 5, 1932.

22. Robertson, *Christian Sisterhood, Race Relations, and the* YWCA.

23. Cochrane, "Student YWCA," 146; Laville, "'If the Time Is Not Ripe'"; Lewis, "Young Women's Christian Association," 72.

24. Laville, "'If the Time Is Not Ripe,'" 361.

25. Robertson, *Christian Sisterhood, Race Relations, and the* YWCA, 16.

26. Sartorius, *Deans of Women and the Feminist Movement*, 122.

27. Cochrane, "Student YWCA," 148.

28. "Confidential: Some Reasons for Giving to the Budget of the National Student Council," November 5, 1924, box 90-10, folder 193, LDS Papers.

29. Slowe, "Higher Education of Negro Women," 356.

30. Cochrane, "Student YWCA," 148.

31. "Report of Commission on Standards," May 5, 1924, box 90-10, folder 193, LDS Papers.

32. Laville, "'If the Time Is Not Ripe,'" 364.

33. Miller and Pruitt-Logan, *Faithful to the Task at Hand*, 277. See also Slowe to President J. Durkee, "Outline of the Duties of the Dean of Women," December 9, 1925, box 90-2, folder 52, LDS Papers.

34. Slowe to Leslie Blanchard, executive secretary, National Student Council, YWCA, February 11, 1925, box 90-2, folder 29, LDS Papers. See also "Women Discuss Causes of War in Conference," *Norfolk (Va.) Journal and Guide*, February 7, 1925.

35. A white woman, Leslie Blanchard had worked with the YWCA as an undergraduate and served as Stanford's chapter president. "YWCA Cabinets Will Hear Leslie Blanchard,

'12," *Daily Palo Alto*, November 28, 1922. She held a master's from the University of Chicago and became executive secretary of the National Student Council of the YWCA. "Dean Blanchard Speaks Before Duke Audience," *Hollins Student Life*, March 10, 1937, https://digitalcommons.hollins.edu/cgi/viewcontent.cgi?article=1109&context =newspapers. In 1935 she was appointed dean at Hollins College and left in 1939 to complete her doctoral degree in the philosophy of education at Columbia University. "Change in Administration," *Hollins Student Life*, March 16, 1939, https://digitalcommons.hollins .edu/cgi/viewcontent.cgi?article=1132&context=newspapers.

36. Slowe to Leslie Blanchard, executive secretary, National Student Council, YWCA, February 11, 1925, box 90-2, folder 29, LDS Papers.

37. "Dean Slowe a Speaker at Columbia U," *Baltimore Afro-American*, January 31, 1925.

38. Lauren Kientz Anderson, "Jumping Overboard: Interpreting Evidence about Same Sex-Love," outhistory, n.d., http://outhistory.org/exhibits/show/juliette-derricotte /derricotte-biography.

39. Robertson, *Christian Sisterhood, Race Relations, and the* YWCA, 134.

40. Slowe to Juliette Derricotte, November 11, 1924, box 90-2, folder 45, LDS Papers.

41. Slowe to Leslie Blanchard, March 19, 1925, box 90-2, folder 29, LDS Papers; "University Notes," 137; "Drive at Howard U. Aided by Churches," *Sunday Star* (Washington, D.C.), April 5, 1925, pt. 1.

42. Slowe to Leslie Blanchard, March 19, 1925.

43. "Woman Educator Foresees Great Future for Co-Eds," March 1, 1931, *Detroit News*, box 90-11, folder 210, LDS Papers.

44. "H.U. Women Students Honor Dean Slowe," *Baltimore Afro-American*, March 21, 1931.

45. Slowe to Thyrsa Amos, March 4, 1931, box 90-2, folder 23, LDS Papers.

46. Nicholas Murray Butler, "Evidences of an Education," *Columbia Spectator*, March 2, 1931.

47. "University Notes," 430; "Visit of Dean Amos," *Hilltop*, May 15, 1930; "One-Day Institute Conducted by Dean Thyrsa W. Amos, Dean of Women, University of Pittsburgh," April 25, 1936, transcript in box 90-6, folder 137, LDS Papers.

48. "One-Day Institute Conducted by Dean."

49. Ibid.

50. Ibid., emphasis added.

51. "Eagles Mere Division of the National Student Council," June 29, 1923, box 90-10, folder 192, LDS Papers.

52. Glembocki, "They Might Be Giants," 21.

53. "One-Day Institute Conducted by Dean."

54. Ibid.

55. Slowe to Thyrsa Amos, June 26, 1936, box 90-2, folder 24, LDS Papers.

56. Brett et al., "A Symposium," 53.

57. Heath, "Our Heritage Speaks." Although Heath was responsible for the convention's logistics, she had inherited the New Orleans site. Heath estimated that Black deans in the NADW numbered about twenty in 1937. "Kathryn G. Heath Oral History Inter-

view," John F. Kennedy Library, JFK#1, June 29, 1971, https://www.jfklibrary.org/sites
/default/files/archives/JFKOH/Heath%2C%20Kathryn%20G/JFKOH-KGH-01
/JFKOH-KGH-01
-TR.pdf. The proceedings of the NADW's 1937 annual meeting list about 950 members
overall. See National Association of Deans of Women, "Membership List."

58. Correspondent, "National Association of Deans of Women," 238; Farley, "Societies
and Meetings: New Orleans," 98.

59. Farley, "Societies and Meetings: Program," 238; Farley, "Superintendents at New
Orleans," 353.

60. Farley, "Superintendents at New Orleans," 354; Farley, "Societies and Meetings:
Program," 237.

61. "Educational Notes and News," 182; Slowe to Irma Voigt, NADW president, Ohio
University, December 3, 1936, box 90-4, folder 96, LDS Papers. Referring to statements by
the boycotting organizations, the African American historian and educator Horace Mann
Bond (1904–1972) excoriated the conference's comfort with segregation. The nostalgia
for slavery was particularly odious because the NEA's Department of Superintendence had
touted the centennial celebration of Horace Mann (1796–1859), the public school champion, inaugural president of Antioch College, and abolitionist. Bond reminded his peers
of the broader principles of justice to which Mann had subscribed and that were blatantly
violated during an educational gathering where "imitation Negro 'mammies' furnished in-
cidental entertainment and real Negro 'mammies' did the dirty work." A final violation
of Mann's educational principles, as Bond pointed out, was that the "souvenir pictorial
booklet" presented to all attendees included "no slightest reference to the existence of Negro children or schools." Bond, "Horace Mann in New Orleans," 607, 610.

62. This was Heath's first convention as executive secretary, a position she held from
1936 to 1943. Heath, "Our Heritage Speaks," 17.

63. Ibid., 19.

64. Ibid..

65. "Kathryn G. Heath Oral History Interview."

66. Heath, "Our Heritage Speaks," 20.

67. Ibid.

68. Voigt, "National Association of Deans of Women," 754.

69. Slowe to Leslie Blanchard, Dean, Hollins College, November 12, 1936, box 90-2,
folder 29, LDS Papers.

70. Ibid.

71. Leslie Blanchard to Slowe, November 23, 1936, box 2, folder 29, LDS Papers.

72. Slowe to Irma Voigt, NADW president, Ohio University, December 3, 1936, box 90-
4, folder 96, LDS Papers.

73. Kathryn G. Heath to Slowe, January 7, 1937, box 90-3, folder 63, LDS Papers.

74. Hilda A. Davis to Slowe, February 16, 1937, box 90-2, folder 43, LDS Papers.

75. Slowe to Hilda Davis, March 3, 1937, box 90-2, folder 43, LDS Papers.

76. The National Association of Deans of Women was founded in 1916 and changed its
name in 1956 to the National Association of Women Deans and Counselors. In 1973 the

NAWDC became the National Association of Women Deans, Administrators, and Counselors. From 1991 to 2000 the professional organization existed as the National Association for Women in Education. In 2000 it merged with the National Association of Student Personnel Administrators. Bashaw, "Reassessment and Redefinition," 158.

77. Brett et al., "A Symposium," 54.
78. Ibid., 53.
79. Ibid.
80. Ibid., 46, 47, 48.
81. Ibid., 49; Heath, "Our Heritage Speaks," 19.
82. Brett et al., "A Symposium," 51.
83. Sartorius, *Deans of Women and the Feminist Movement*, 122.
84. Brett et al., "A Symposium," 46.
85. Record of the friends who called and the flowers received in the funeral of Lucy D. Slowe, box 90-1, folder 18, LDS Papers.
86. Program, National Association of College Women Annual Meeting, April 15–17, 1938, Pittsburgh, box 90-1, folder 10, LDS Papers. See also "Convention Moves Smoothly Through Pleasant Weekend," *Pittsburgh Courier*, April 23, 1938.
87. Miller and Pruitt-Logan, *Faithful to the Task at Hand*, 330.
88. Ibid.

Chapter 4. Our Dean, Our Selves

The Burrill letter quoted in the epigraph appears in box 90-2, folder 35, LDS Papers; the headline on the *Baltimore Afro-American* article was "Miss Slowe Says Dean's Job Is Hard One to Fill."

1. "Women's Dean Job Is Not Campus Housekeeper—Slowe," *Baltimore Afro-American*, April 6, 1935; "'Women's Deans Not Lady Cops'—Dean Slowe," *Chicago Defender*, April 4, 1936; Slowe, "Place of the Dean of Women on the College Campus," 51.
2. Slowe, "The Role of the Dean of Women in the Academic Life of the College," March 1935, box 90-6, folder 142, LDS Papers.
3. Lindsey, *Colored No More*, 51.
4. Heldke, "A DuBoisian Proposal."
5. Gaines, *Uplifting the Race*, 25.
6. Ibid.
7. Locke, *New Negro*, 3, 15.
8. Pochmara, *Making of the New Negro*, 60; Chapman, *Prove It on Me*, 4.
9. Ross, *Manning the Race*; Curwood, *Stormy Weather*.
10. Locke, *New Negro*, 3, 4.
11. Chapman, *Prove It on Me*, 57.
12. Waite, "DuBois and the Invisible Talented Tenth"; Plastas, *A Band of Noble Women*.
13. McDougald, "Task of Negro Womanhood," 372, 380–81; McDougald, "Double Task."
14. Slowe to Abraham Flexner, August 1, 1933, box 90-13, folder 234, LDS Papers.
15. Perkins, "National Association of College Women."

16. Slowe to J. Stanley Durkee, May 31, 1922, box 90-2, folder 51, LDS Papers. A copy of this letter also appears in "Memorandum for Mrs. Marian Bannister in re: case of Lucy D. Slowe, A.B. Howard; M.A. Columbia, Dean of Women at Howard University," box 90-1, folder 1, LDS Papers.

17. Karen Anderson, "From 'Brickbats and Roses,'" 285.

18. Burrill was a familiar guest of the Women's Department, Slowe's office and the robust social curriculum it developed with Howard women students. Burrill helped organize the Christmas Vesper service that Slowe introduced to the campus, and was also the conservator of Slowe's papers, which she annotated and withheld from Howard University. Slowe's materials were initially deposited at Morgan State College (now University), which donated them to Howard in 1966. Greta A. Wilson, Finding Aid for Lucy Diggs Slowe Papers, June 1980, https://dh.howard.edu/cgi/viewcontent.cgi?article=1174 &context=finaid_manu.

19. "Historical Preservation Review Board Application for Historic Landmark or Historic District Designation for Slowe-Burrill House," December 2019, https://planning .dc.gov/sites/default/files/dc/sites/op/publication/attachments/Slowe%20Burrill%20 House%20nomination_0.pdf.

20. Slowe to Flexner, June 2, 1933, and August 1, 1933, box 90-3, folder 58, LDS Papers.

21. Slowe to Flexner, August 1, 1933; "Memorandum for Mrs. Marian Bannister in re: case of Lucy D. Slowe," ca. 1933, box 90-1, folder 1, LDS Papers.

22. Valarie O'Mega Justiss to Miss Walker, November 5, 1938, box 90-1, folder 3, LDS Papers.

23. These garden parties are noted in the *Evening Star* of Washington, D.C., from 1929 to 1935. See, for example, "Howard U. Plans for Graduation," May 26, 1929; "Howard Plans Reception," June 4, 1933; "Freedman Nurses Graduate Tonight," June 4, 1935.

24. Mina Kerr to J. Stanley Durkee, June 26, 1925, box 90-2, folder 52, LDS Papers. According to Slowe's biographers, the budget committee of the board of trustees decided that she should live in Miner Hall "to better protect the young women especially during the evenings and nights when watchful care is most needed and that she be requested to do so." Miller and Pruitt-Logan, *Faithful to the Task at Hand*, 124.

25. Kerr to Durkee, June 26, 1925.

26. McKinney, "Mordecai Johnson."

27. "New Orders to Dean Lucy Slowe at Howard Termed Persecution," *Baltimore Afro-American*, July 22,1933.

28. "Additions to the Faculty, 1922–1923," 45.

29. "Memorandum on the Mills Case: Statement made by L.D. Slowe," May 1933, box 90-5, folder 116, LDS Papers.

30. Clarence Harvey Mills to Slowe, January 11, 1927, box 90-3, folder 80, LDS Papers.

31. Brittney C. Cooper, *Beyond Respectability*, 88; Mills to Slowe, January 11, 1927.

32. "Memorandum on the Mills Case." .

33. Clarence Harvey Mills to Slowe, January 13, 1927, box 90-3, folder 80, LDS Papers.

34. "Memorandum on the Mills Case." See also "Howard Drops Prof. Mills, Appoints 4 Instructors," *Baltimore Afro-American*, July 30, 1927. The article says that "while no

authoritative facts could be obtained, it is alleged by those who are familiar with the affairs of the university that Prof. Mills was charged with unseemly conduct in his classroom while the co-eds were present and likewise a misunderstanding with the Dean of Women."

35. "Memorandum on the Mills Case."

36. Ibid.

37. Slowe to "Members of the Board of Trustees, Howard University," April 26, 1933, box 90-5, folder 113, LDS Papers.

38. Mary P. Burrill, "Note," box 90-3, folder 80, LDS Papers.

39. Slowe to President Johnson, February 28, 1931, box 90-3, folder 71, LDS Papers.

40. Slowe to Professor Ralph J. Bunche, November 2, 1931, box 90-2, folder 34, LDS Papers.

41. Kelly Miller to Mordecai Johnson, February 9, 1932, box 90-3, folder 72, LDS Papers.

42. Slowe, "1936–1937 Annual Report of the Dean of Women addressed to President Johnson," June 30, 1937, box 90-5, folder 114, LDS Papers.

43. "Miller Urges Howard to Honor Dean Slowe," *Baltimore Afro-American*, November 6, 1937.

44. Johnson to Slowe, February 16, 1933, box 90-3, folder 73, LDS Papers.

45. Slowe to board of trustees, April 26, 1933, box 90-5, folder 113, LDS Papers. In her 1937 annual report, the last of her tenure, Slowe listed the following as her staff—Joanna Houston, assistant to the dean of women, director of Frazier Hall, and part-time instructor in English; Eva B. Holmes, director of Crandall Hall; Alida P. Banks, assistant director of Frazier Hall; and Willie B. Wilson, secretary.

46. Joanna Houston, "Annual Report of the Assistant to the Dean of Women, 1932–1933," box 90-5, folder 114, LDS Papers.

47. Slowe to Mr. V. D. Johnson, Howard University treasurer, January 11, 1934, box 90-3, folder 74, LDS Papers.

48. Joanna R. Houston, assistant to the dean of women, to Slowe, January 3, 1934, box 90-3, folder 65, LDS Papers.

49. "Memo Re: Grievances Submitted by Women Students in the Dormitories on the Dining Department," n.d., box 90-5, folder 113, LDS Papers.

50. "Memorandum to President Johnson in re: The Women Students' Protest Against the Dismissal of Dr. Dorothy Boulding," May 12, 1933, box 90-3, folder 57. See also "Howard U. Coeds Ask That Woman Doctor Be Retained," *Baltimore Afro-American*, May 13, 1933.

51. "Howard U. Coeds Ask. "See also Slowe memo to Johnson, May 12, 1933, box 90-5, folder 113, LDS Papers.

52. Flexner (1866–1959), a reformer of medical schools and higher education in general, was named to the Howard University Board of Trustees in 1930, the same year he began heading the Institute for Advanced Study in New York City (1930–39). He became the board chair on April 19, 1932, and resigned in March 1935. Miller and Pruitt-Logan, *Faithful to the Task at Hand*, 169, 213.

53. "Howard Women Rebuke Trustee Board Head," *Baltimore Afro-American*, week of May 13, 1933, box 90-13, folder 234, LDS Papers.

54. Ibid.

55. Flexner to Slowe, May 12, 1933, box 90-3, folder 57, LDS Papers.

56. Slowe to Flexner, May 20, 1933, box 90-3, folder 57, LDS Papers.

57. Howard alumnae to Jesse E. Moorland, chairman, Executive Committee of Board of Trustees of Howard University, undated (ca. 1933), box 90-3, folder 81, LDS Papers.

58. Charlotte Atwood to the board of trustees, September 25, 1933, box 90-2, folder 25, LDS Papers.

59. "New Orders to Dean Lucy Slowe at Howard Termed Persecution," *Baltimore Afro-American*, July 22, 1933. Alumnae letter "To Members of the Board of Trustees of Howard University," n.d., box 90-5, folder 113, LDS Papers.

60. Slowe to Johnson, June 26, 1933, box 90-3, folder 73, LDS Papers.

61. "H.U. Reorganization Wipes Out Reasons Assigned for New Buildings," *Baltimore Afro-American*, July 29, 1933.

62. "Only a New Administration Can Save Howard University," *Baltimore Afro-American*, August 12, 1933.

63. "15 of Howard's Faculty May Be Dropped in June," *Baltimore Afro-American*, April 22, 1933.

64. Slowe to George W. Crawford, June 30, 1933, box 90-2, folder 41, LDS Papers.

65. Miller and Pruitt-Logan, *Faithful to the Task at Hand*, 189.

66. Slowe to Crawford, August 17, 1933, box 90-2, folder 41, LDS Papers.

67. Ibid.

68. Lamb, *Howard University Medical Department*, 261; "The Horizon," 277; Barber, "Philadelphia Negro Dentist"; "Dr. W. M. Slowe Dead," *Evening Journal* (Wilmington, Delaware), August 21, 1923.

69. Slowe to Crawford, August 17, 1933.

70. Slowe to Johnson, September 22, 1933, box 90-3, folder 73, LDS Papers.

71. Daniel Calhoun Roper (1867–1943) served as secretary of commerce from 1933 to 1938 in FDR's administration. Carter Glass (1858–1946) served as U.S. senator from Virginia from 1920 to 1946. He chaired the Senate Appropriations Committee from 1933 to 1946.

72. "Memo for Mrs. Marian Bannister in re: case of Lucy D. Slowe," 1933, box 90-1, folder 1, LDS Papers.

73. Rasheed (*Lucy Diggs Slowe*, 187) cites Rayford Logan's institutional history (*Howard University*, 292) and his claim that in mid-September 1933, Johnson relented on his insistence that Slowe occupy university housing because she had an illness.

74. Eva M. Holmes, Juanita P. Howard, Coralie F. Cook, Charlotte Atwood, and Alice Nelson Williams to Dr. Abraham Flexner, October 4, 1933, box 90-3, folder 59, LDS Papers.

75. "H.U. Trustees Refuse Coeds' Petition," *Baltimore Afro-American*, November 4, 1933.

76. "Howard Women at 12th Dinner," *Baltimore Afro-American*, November 4, 1933.

77. "Howard Women Hold Twelfth Annual Dinner," *Pittsburgh Courier*, November 18, 1933, box 90-13, folder 234, LDS Papers.

78. "Memorandum on the Department of the Dean of Women Howard University," October 9, 1933, box 90-3, folder 73, LDS Papers. Slowe's final salary increase of $200 was awarded in July 1935. Miller and Pruitt-Logan, *Faithful the Task at Hand*, 213. As dean of women, she never matched the $4,000 salary she had left as principal of Shaw in 1922.

79. Slowe, 1936–1937 annual report, June 30, 1937.

80. Johnson to Slowe, August 20, 1937, and Slowe to Johnson, August 25, 1937, box 90-3, folder 73, LDS Papers.

81. Miller and Pruitt-Logan, *Faithful to the Task at Hand*, 231.

82. Kathryn G. Heath to Slowe, September 8, 1937, box 90-3, folder 63, and Joanna Houston to Slowe, September 6, 1937, box 90-3, folder 65, both in LDS Papers.

83. Slowe to Joanna Houston, July 21, 1937, box 90-3, folder 65, LDS Papers.

84. "Seriously Ill," *Baltimore Afro-American*, September 18, 1937.

85. "Dean Slowe Still on Very Sick List," *Baltimore Afro-American*, October 2, 1937.

86. "Death-Bed Ultimatum," 3; "Howard Trustees Get Ouster Plea," *Evening Star*, October 27, 1937.

87. "Deaths," *Evening Star*, October 22, 1937.

88. "The Death-Bed Ultimatum"; "She Has Not Died in Vain."

89. "Flash: Dean Slowe Buried from H.U. Chapel," *Baltimore Afro-American*, October 30, 1937. A dispatch in Slowe's papers from the Capital News Service, a Black weekly news agency in Washington, D.C., bears the headline "Regret Expressed That President and Trustees of Howard Did Not Appreciate Dean Slowe." The story, dated November 8, 1937, points out that "it is generally believed that the stress and strain under which Dean Slowe worked at Howard during the last three or four years contributed largely to her untimely death"(see box 90-1, folder 9, in Slowe's papers).

90. Mordecai Johnson to Nellie Hawkes, October 24, 1937, box 90-1, folder 3, LDS Papers.

91. "Directors for Girls Are Appointed Here," *Hilltop*, September 29, 1937.

92. "Puh-lease, Miss Banks," *Hilltop*, October 13, 1937.

93. "Dean Lucy Slowe," *Hilltop*, October 27, 1937.

94. "Dean Lucy D. Slowe Passes Away Following Illness of Three Months," *Hilltop*, October 27, 1937; "Office: Dean of Women," *Hilltop*, November 10, 1937.

95. "Says Dean Slowe Dies as Martyr," *Afro-American*, October 30, 1937, Washington ed.

Conclusion

The eulogy may be found in box 90-1, folder 1, LDS Papers.

1. Burrill to T. L. Hungate, chairman, Howard University Board of Trustees, October 30, 1937, box 90-1, folder 3, LDS Papers.

2. "Kelly Miller Writes about the Passing of an Eminent Woman," *New York Age*, November 6, 1937.

3. Ella L. Murphy to Mary Burrill, December 2, 1937, box 90-1, folder 3, LDS Papers.

4. "A Tribute to Soror Lucy D. Slowe," 34.

5. Brenda Franke to Mary Burrill, December 15, 1937, box 90-1, folder 3, LDS Papers.

6. Hilda A. Davis, "Howard Women's Dinner Speech," November 7, 1941, box 90-1, folder 9, LDS Papers.

7. Western Union telegram of condolence to Mary Burrill from AKA Sorority sent by Le Claire Knox and Jennie Young, October 24, 1937, box 90-1, folder 5, LDS Papers.

8. Verna Dozier, "Challenge: To the Memory of Dean Slowe," December 1937, box 90-1, folder 9, LDS Papers.

9. "Dr. Philips Addresses Howard," *Evening Star* (Washington, D.C.), October 25, 1931; Ketura Whitehurst to Mary Burrill, November 9, 1937, box 90-1, folder 3, LDS Papers.

10. Marion Wright to Mary Burrill, November 6, 1937, box 90-1, folder 3, LDS Papers.

11. *Journal of the College Alumnae Club of Washington*, January 1939.

12. "Dear Howardites and Friends," March 29, 1943, box 90-1, folder 3, LDS Papers. See also "Late Dean of Women, Lucy Diggs Slowe, Honored by University," *Pittsburgh Courier*, November 13, 1943.

13. From 1942 to 1955 the Howard University Women's Club of Washington, D.C., hosted the dinner, and in 1956, the Dean of Women's Office sponsored the event. "200 HU Women Return for Yearly Weekend on Campus," *Baltimore Afro-American*, November 17, 1956. In 1947 the alumnae group celebrated the event's silver anniversary, and in 1954 this group made the dinner the opening event of a three-day weekend. "Howard Women Plan for Year," *Baltimore Afro-American*, October 9, 1954. Several distinguished Black women attended, including Dr. Mamie Clark, a Howard graduate and founder and director of New York City's Northside Center for Child Development, who gave the keynote address; Jeanne Noble, dean of women at Oklahoma's Langston University; Bertha McNeill, Slowe's Howard classmate, an AKA soror, and president of the Washington, D.C., chapter of the Women's International League for Peace and Freedom; and Vivian Cook, a 1912 Howard University alumna and principal of Baltimore's Dunbar High School. "College Women Hold First Week End Meet at Howard U," *Baltimore Afro-American*, November 6, 1954.

14. "Mrs. Murphy Addresses Howard Women's Club," *Baltimore Afro-American*, November 19, 1955.

15. Ibid.

16. Simmons, *Crescent City Girls*, 190.

17. "Mrs. Murphy Addresses."

18. Ibid.

19. For an analysis that draws parallels between Slowe's work and Black girl magic, see Yeboah, "Blueprint for Black Girl Magic."

20. Simmons, *Crescent City Girls*, 5.

21. Slowe, "Address Delivered by Soror Lucy D. Slowe," 20.

22. Hilda A. Davis, "Howard Women's Dinner Speech," November 7, 1941, box 90-1, folder 9, LDS Papers.

BIBLIOGRAPHY

Archival Sources

Lucy Diggs Slowe Papers. Boxes 90-1 to 90-15. Moorland-Spingarn Research Center, Howard University, Washington, D.C.

Books, Articles, and Documents

Addams, Jane. *Newer Ideals of Peace.* 1922; repr., Urbana: University of Illinois Press, 2007.

"Additions to the Faculty, 1922–1923." *Howard University Record* 17.1 (1922): 45.

"Among the Many Interesting Adjuncts to the University." *Howard University Journal* 17.6 (1923): 333–34.

Amos, Thyrsa. "Unsocial Aspects of the Social Curriculum." *Teaching* 6.5 (1922): 5–18.

Amott, Teresa, and Julie Matthaei. *Race, Gender, and Work: A Multi-Cultural Economic History of Women in the United States.* Boston: South End Press, 1999.

Anderson, Karen. "Brickbats and Roses: Lucy Diggs Slowe, 1883–1937." In *Lone Voyagers: Academic Women in Coeducational Institutions, 1870–1937.* Edited by Geraldine Joncich Clifford, 283–307. New York: Feminist Press, 1989.

Anderson, Karen. "From 'Brickbats and Roses': Lucy Diggs Slowe, 1883–1937." *Women's Studies Quarterly* 22.1/2 (1994): 134–40.

Anderson, Monica. "A Look at Historically Black Colleges and Universities as Howard Turns 150." FactTank, February 28, 2017. https://www.pewresearch.org/fact-tank/2017/02/28/a-look-at-historically-black-colleges-and-universities-as-howard-turns-150/.

"Annual Congressional Appropriation of $500,000 Suggested." *Howard University Record* 19.6 (1925): 295.

Bailey, Alison. "Locating Traitorous Identities: Toward a Theory of White Character Formation." *Hypatia* 13.3 (1998): 27–42.

Bair, Sarah D. "Educating Black Girls in the Early 20th Century: The Pioneering Work of Nannie Helen Burroughs (1879–1961)." *Theory and Research in Social Education,* 36.1 (2008): 9–35.

Barber, J. Max. "The Philadelphia Negro Dentist." *Crisis: A Record of the Darker Races* 7.4 (1914): 179–81.

Bashaw, Carolyn Terry. "Reassessment and Redefinition: The NAWDC and Higher Education for Women." In *Women Administrators in Higher Education: Historical and Contemporary Perspectives.* Edited by Jana Nidiffer and Carolyn Terry Bashaw, 157–182. Albany, N.Y.: SUNY Press, 2001.

Bashaw, Carolyn Terry. *Stalwart Women: A Historical Analysis of Deans of Women in the South.* New York: Teachers College Press, 1999.

Bell-Scott, Patricia. "The Business of Being a Dean of Women." *Initiatives* 54.2 (1991): 35–41.

Bell-Scott, Patricia. "'To Keep My Self-Respect': Dean Lucy Diggs Slowe's 1927 Memorandum on the Sexual Harassment of Black Women." *NWSA Journal* 9.2 (1997): 70–76.

Bertaux, Nancy E., and M. Christine Anderson. "An Emerging Tradition of Educational Achievement: African American Women in College and the Professions, 1920–1950." *Equity & Excellence in Education* 34.2 (2001): 16–21.

Blackwell-Johnson, Joyce. "African American Activists in the Women's International League for Peace and Freedom, 1920s–1950s." *Peace & Change* 23.4 (1998): 466–82.

Blanding, Sarah G. "Between Us Talk." *Journal of the National Association of Women Deans, Administrators, and Counselors* (winter 1986): 8–13.

Blitz, Anne Dudley. "Social Conditions Arising from Inter-Racial Contacts on the Campus." In *Report of the Tenth Annual Meeting of National Association of Deans of Women,* 73–79. Washington, D.C.: National Association of Deans of Women, 1923.

Bond, Horace Mann. "Horace Mann in New Orleans: A Note on the Decline of Humanitarianism in American Education, 1837–1937." *School and Society* 45.1166 (May 1, 1937): 607–11.

Bordin, Ruth. *Alice Freeman Palmer: The Evolution of a New Woman.* Ann Arbor: University of Michigan, 1993.

Brett, Ruth, Edna M. Calhoun, Lucille J. Piggott, Hilda A. Davis, and Patricia Bell Scott. "A Symposium: Our Living History: Reminiscences of Black Participation in NAWDAC." *Journal of* NAWDAC 49.2 (Winter 1986): 46–56.

Brown, Maude E. "The College Woman Accepts the Challenge." *Alpha Kappa Alpha Ivy Leaf* (March 1938): 5–6.

Chapman, Erin D. *Prove It on Me: New Negroes, Sex, and Popular Culture in the 1920s.* New York: Oxford University Press, 2012.

Chatelain, Marcia. *South Side Girls: Growing Up in the Great Migration.* Durham, N.C.: Duke University Press, 2015.

Cochrane, Sharlene Voogd. "The Student YWCA: Intersections of Gender, Religion, and Race, 1915–1924." In *Educational Work of Women's Organizations, 1890–1960.* Edited by Anne Meis Knupfer and Christine Woyshner, 143–162. New York: Palgrave Macmillan, 2008.

Cole, Johnnetta, and Beverly Guy-Sheftall. *Gender Talk: The Struggle for Women's Equality in African American Communities*. New York: One World Books, 2003.

"College of Arts and Sciences, Graduating Class of 1908." *Howard University Record* 2.4 (November 1908): 2. https://babel.hathitrust.org/cgi/pt?id=uiuo.ark:/13960/t2g74q41k.

"College Women Hold First Week End Meet at Howard U." *Baltimore Afro-American*, November 6, 1954.

Combahee River Collective. "The Combahee River Collective Statement." 1977. https://americanstudies.yale.edu/sites/default/files/files/Keyword%20Coalition_Readings.pdf.

Cooper, Anna Julia. "The Higher Education of Women." In Lemert and Bhan, *Voice of Anna Julia Cooper*, 72–87.

Cooper, Anna Julia. "The Intellectual Progress of the Colored Women in the United States since the Emancipation Proclamation: A Response to Fannie Barrier Williams." 1893. In Lemert and Bhan, *Voice of Anna Julia Cooper*, 201–205.

Cooper, Anna Julia. "The Status of Woman in America." 1892. In Lemert and Bhan, *Voice of Anna Julia Cooper*, 109–17.

Cooper, Brittney C. *Beyond Respectability: The Intellectual Thought of Race Women*. Chicago: University of Illinois Press, 2017.

Correspondent. "The National Association of Deans of Women." *School and Society* 45.1155 (1937): 238–39.

Crocco, Margaret Smith, and Cally L. Waite. "Education and Marginality: Race and Gender in Higher Education, 1940–1955." *History of Education Quarterly* 47.1 (2007): 69–91.

Cromwell, Mary E. "The Proposed National Federation." *Proceedings of the Conference of College Women Called by the College Alumnae Club of Washington, D.C., April 6 and 7, 1923*, no. 1. Washington, D.C.: Association of College Women, 1923.

Crump, Charlotte. "This Free North." *Opportunity: Journal of Negro Life* 15.9 (September 1937): 271–72, 285.

Curwood, Anastasia. "A Fresh Look at E. Franklin Frazier's Sexual Politics in *The Negro Family in the United States*." *DuBois Review* 5.2 (2008): 325–37.

Curwood, Anastasia C. *Stormy Weather: Middle-Class African American Marriages Between the Two World Wars*. Chapel Hill: University of North Carolina Press, 2010.

Cuthbert, Marion. "Letter of Condolences." *Journal of the College Alumnae Club of Washington*, memorial ed. (January 1939): 70–71.

Daniel, Walter G. "A Tribute to Marion Thompson Wright." *Journal of Negro Education* 32.3 (1963): 308–10.

Davis, Hilda A. "It Gives Me Great Pleasure." *Journal of the College Alumnae Club of Washington*, memorial ed. (January 1939): 72–73.

Davis, Hilda A., and Patricia Bell-Scott. "Association of Deans of Women and Advisers to Girls in Negro Schools." In *Black Women in America: An Historical Encyclopedia*. Edited by Darlene Clark Hine, 49–51. 1st ed. New York: Carlson, 1993.

Davis, Hilda, and Patricia Bell-Scott. "The Association of Deans of Women and Advisers to Girls in Negro Schools, 1929–1954: A Brief Oral History." *Sage: A Scholarly Journal on Black Women* 6.1 (1989): 40–44.

"The Dean of Women Talked to Men." *Howard University Record* 17.1 (1922): 51–52.

"Dean Slowe Speaks at National Association of Deans of Women." *Howard University Record* 17.6 (1923): 334.

"The Death-Bed Ultimatum." *Howard University Alumni Journal: The Case Against President Mordecai W. Johnson* (winter 1937): 3.

Deegan, Mary Jo, ed. *The Collected Writings of Fannie Barrier Williams, 1893–1918.* DeKalb: Northern Illinois University Press, 2002.

"The Delta Sigma Theta Sorority House." *Howard University Record* 17.2 (1922): 90.

Dotson, Kristie. "Theorizing Jane Crow, Theorizing Unknowability." *Social Epistemology* 31.5 (2017): 417–30.

Du Bois, W. E. B. *The Souls of Black Folk: Essays and Sketches.* Chicago: A. C. McClurg, 1903.

Duffy, Jennifer. "How Women Impacted the Historical Development of Student Affairs." *College Student Affairs Journal* 28.2 (2010): 235–50.

"Educational Notes and News." *School and Society,* 45.1154 (February 6, 1937): 179–83.

Evans, Stephanie Y. *Black Women in the Ivory Tower, 1850–1954: An Intellectual History.* Gainesville: University Press of Florida, 2007.

Farley, Belmont. "Societies and Meetings: The New Orleans Convention of the Department of Superintendence." *School and Society* 45.1151 (January 16, 1937): 98–100.

Farley, Belmont. "Societies and Meetings: Program for the New Orleans Meeting." *School and Society* 45.1155 (February 13, 1937): 237–38.

Farley, Belmont. "The Superintendents at New Orleans." *School and Society* 45.1159 (March 13, 1937): 353–61.

"The First Annual Howard Women's Dinner." *Howard University Record* 17.2 (1922): 88–90.

Fleming, Jacqueline. "Black Women in Black and White College Environments: The Making of a Matriarch." *Journal of Social Issues* 39.3 (1983): 41–54.

Gaines, Kevin K. *Uplifting the Race: Black Leadership, Politics, and Culture in the Twentieth Century.* Chapel Hill: University of North Carolina Press, 1996.

Gaston-Gayles, J., L. Wolf-Wendel, S. Twonbly, K. Ward, and K. Tuttle. "From Disciplinarian to Change Agent: How the Civil Rights Era Changed the Roles of Student Affairs Professionals." *NASPA Journal* 42.3 (2005): 263–82.

Glembocki, Vicki. "They Might Be Giants." *Pitt Magazine* 10.6 (December 1995): 19–25. https://www.gsws.pitt.edu/sites/default/files/95.12_-_pitt_magazine.they_might_be_giants.celebrating_the_100yr_anniversary_of_women_at_pitt.pdf.

Graham, Patricia Albjerg. "Women in Academe." *Science,* New Series 169.3952 (1970): 1284–90.

Guy-Sheftall, Beverly. *Daughters of Sorrow: Attitudes Toward Black Women, 1880–1920.* Vol. 11 of Black Women in United States History Series. New York: Carlson, 1990.

Haidarali, Laila. "The New Negro Woman Goes to Campus: Gender, Generation and Interwar African American Womanhood," Research Papers No. 5. Department of History, University of Essex, 2013. http://repository.essex.ac.uk/7680/1/RP5-Haidarali-2013.pdf.

Harley, Sharon. "Beyond the Classroom: The Organization Lives of Black Female Educators in the District of Columbia, 1890–1930." *Journal of Negro Education* 51.3 (1982): 254–65.

Harley, Sharon. "Nannie Helen Burroughs: 'The Black Goddess of Liberty.'" *Journal of Negro History* 81.1/4 (1996): 62–71.

Harper, Frances Ellen Watkins. "Woman's Political Future—Address by Frances E. W. Harper of Virginia." In *The World's Congress of Representative Women*. Edited by May Wright Sewall, 433–37. Chicago: Rand McNally, 1894.

Haynes, Chayla, Nicole M. Joseph, Lori D. Patton, Saran Steward, and Evette L. Allen. "Toward an Understanding of Intersectionality Methodology: A 30-Year Literature Synthesis of Black Women's Experiences in Higher Education. *Review of Educational Research* 90.6 (2020): 751–87.

Heath, Kathryn G. "Our Heritage Speaks." *Journal of the National Association of Women Deans, Administrators & Counselors* 49.2 (1986): 14–21.

Heldke, Lisa. "A DuBoisian Proposal for Persistently White Colleges." *Journal of Speculative Philosophy* 18.3 (2004): 224–38.

Hevel, Michael S. "Toward a History of Student Affairs: A Synthesis of Research, 1996–2015." *Journal of College Student Development* 57.7 (2016): 844–62.

Higginbotham, Evelyn Brooks. *Righteous Discontent: The Women's Movement in the Black Baptist Church, 1880–1920*. Cambridge, Mass.: Harvard University Press, 1994.

Hine, Darlene Clark. "Rape and the Inner Lives of Black Women in the Middle West." *Signs* 14.4 (1989): 912–20.

Holmes, Dwight Oliver Wendell. *The Evolution of the Negro College*. 1934; repr., New York: AMS Press, 1970.

"The Horizon." *Crisis: A Record of the Darker Races* 26.6 (October 1923): 277.

Horowitz, Helen Lefkowitz. *Campus Life: Undergraduate Cultures from the End of the Eighteenth Century to the Present*. Chicago: University of Chicago, 1988.

"Howard Women Hold First Annual Dinner in University's New Dining Hall." *Howard University Record* 17.2 (1922): 86.

Johnson, Karen A. "Gender and Race: Exploring Anna Julia Cooper's Thoughts for Socially Just Educational Opportunities." *Philosophia Africana* 12.1 (2009): 67–82.

Johnson, Karen A. "'In Service for the Common Good': Anna Julia Cooper and Adult Education." *African American Review* 43.1 (2009): 45–56.

Jones, Charisse, and Kumea Shorter-Gooden. *Shifting: The Double Lives of Black Women in America*. New York: Harper Perennial, 2004.

Jones, Jane Louise. *A Personnel Study of Women Deans in Colleges and Universities*. New York: Teachers College, 1928.

Kennedy, Joy L. "The HBCU Experience: Liberating or Not?" *Urban Review* 44 (2012): 358–77.

Lamb, Daniel Smith. *Howard University Medical Department: A Historical, Biographical and Statistical Souvenir*. Washington, D.C.: R. Beresford, 1900.

Laville, Helen. "'If the Time Is Not Ripe, Then It Is Your Job to Ripen the Time!' The Transformation of the YWCA in the USA from Segregated Association to Interracial Organization, 1930–1965." *Women's History Review* 15.3 (2006): 359–83.

Lemert, Charles, and Esme Bhan, eds. *The Voice of Anna Julia Cooper*. Lanham, Md.: Rowman & Littlefield, 1998.

Lewis, Abigail Sara. "The Young Women's Christian Association's Multiracial Activism in the Immediate Postwar Era." In *Freedom Rights: New Perspectives on the Civil Rights Movement*. Edited by Danielle L. McGuire and John Dittmer, 71–110. Lexington: University of Kentucky, 2011.

Lindsey, Treva B. "Climbing the Hilltop: In Search of a New Negro Womanhood at Howard University." In *Escape from New York: The New Negro Renaissance Beyond Harlem*. Edited by Davarian L. Baldwin and Minkah Makalani, 281–90. Minneapolis: University of Minnesota Press, 2013.

Lindsey, Treva B. *Colored No More: Reinventing Black Womanhood in Washington, D.C.* Urbana: University of Illinois, 2017.

Lindsey, Treva B. "Configuring Modernities: New Negro Womanhood in the Nation's Capital, 1890–1940." Ph.D. diss., Duke University, 2010.

Locke, Alain Le Roy, ed. *The New Negro: An Interpretation*. 1925; repr., New York: Touchstone, 1997.

Logan, Rayford W. *Howard University: The First Hundred Years, 1867–1967*. New York: New York University Press, 1969.

Lounsbury, John H. "Deferred but Not Deterred: A Middle School Manifesto." *Middle School Journal* 40. 5(2009): 31–36.

Lowe, Margaret A. *Looking Good: College Women and Body Image, 1875–1930*. Baltimore: Johns Hopkins University Press, 2003.

MacDonald, J. Ramsey. "American Social Settlements." *Commons* 2 (February 1898): 4–6.

McCluskey, Audrey Thomas. "'We Specialize in the Wholly Impossible': Black Women School Founders and Their Mission." *Signs* 22.2 (1997): 403–26.

McDaniel, Anne, Thomas A. DiPrete, Claudia Buchmann, and Uri Shwed. "The Black Gender Gap in Educational Attainment: Historical Trends and Racial Comparisons." *Demography* 48 (2011): 889–914.

McDougald, Elise. "The Double Task." *Survey* 53 (March 1, 1925): 689–91.

McDougald, Elise Johnson. "The Task of Negro Womanhood." In Locke, *New Negro: An Interpretation*, 68–75.

McKinney, Richard I. "Mordecai Johnson: An Early Pillar of African-American Higher Education." *Journal of Blacks in Higher Education* 27 (2000): 99–104.

Melancon, Trimiko. *Unbought and Unbossed: Transgressive Black Women, Sexuality, and Representation*. Philadelphia: Temple University Press, 2014.

Miller, Carroll L. L., and Anne S. Pruitt-Logan. *Faithful to the Task at Hand: The Life of Lucy Diggs Slowe*. Albany: State University of New York Press, 2012.

National Association of Deans of Women. "Membership List." In *Proceedings of the Annual Meeting of the National Association of Deans of Women, 21st Annual Meeting*, 122–85. Washington, D.C.: National Association of Deans of Women, 1937.

Neale, Mamie Geraldine. "The New Howard Woman." *Howard University Record* 17.1 (1922): 49.

Neverdon-Morton, Cynthia. "Self-Help Programs as Educative Activities of Black Women in the South." *Journal of Negro Education* 51.3 (1982): 207–221.

Newcomer, Mabel. *A Century of Higher Education for American Women.* New York: Harper, 1959.

"New Negro Woman," editorial. *(New York City) Messenger,* July 1923, 757.

Nidiffer, Jana. "Advocates on Campus: Deans of Women Create a New Profession." In Nidiffer and Bashaw, *Women Administrators in Higher Education,* 135–56. Albany, N.Y.: SUNY Press, 2001.

Nidiffer, Jana. "'Crumbs from the Boy's Table': The First Century of Coeducation." In Nidiffer and Bashaw, *Women Administrators in Higher Education,* 13–34.

Nidiffer, Jana, and Carolyn Terry Bashaw, eds. *Women Administrators in Higher Education: Historical and Contemporary Perspectives.* Albany, N.Y.: SUNY Press, 2001.

Njoku, Nadrea, Malika Butler, and Cameron C. Beatty. "Reimagining the Historically Black College and University (HBCU) Environment: Exposing Race Secrets and the Binding Chains of Respectability and Othermothering." *International Journal of Qualitative Studies in Education* 30.8(2017): 783–99.

Noble, Jeanne. "The Higher Education of Black Women in the Twentieth Century." In *Women and Higher Education in American History: Essays from the Mount Holyoke College Sesquicentennial Symposia.* Edited by John Mack Faragher and Florence Howe, 87–106. New York: W. W. Norton, 1988.

Noble, Jeanne. *The Negro Woman's College Education.* New York: Teachers College, 1956.

"Our Dean of Women." *Howard Alumnus,* March 1924, 79.

Palmer, Alice Freeman. "A Review of the Higher Education of Women." *Forum* 12 (September 1891): 28–40.

Palmieri, Patricia Ann. *In Adamless Eden: The Community of Women Faculty at Wellesley.* New Haven, Conn.: Yale University Press, 1995.

Palmieri, Patricia Ann. "Symmetrical Womanhood: The Educational Ideology of Activism at Wellesley." *Academe* 81.4 (1995): 16–20.

Patterson, Martha H. *Beyond the Gibson Girl: Reimagining the American New Woman, 1895–1915.* Urbana: University of Illinois, 2008.

Perkins, Linda M. "The African American Female Elite: The Early History of African American Women in the Seven Sister Colleges, 1880–1960." *Harvard Educational Review* 67.4 (1997): 718–56.

Perkins, Linda M. "The Impact of the 'Cult of True Womanhood' on the Education of Black Women." *Journal of Social Issues* 39.3 (1983): 17–28.

Perkins, Linda M. "Lucy Diggs Slowe: Champion of the Self-Determination of African-American Women in Higher Education." *Journal of Negro History* 81.1/4 (1996): 89–104.

Perkins, Linda M. "The National Association of College Women: Vanguard of Black Women's Leadership and Education, 1923–1954." *Journal of Education* 172.3 (1990): 65–75.

Perkins, Linda M. "The Role of Education in the Development of Black Feminist Thought, 1860–1920." *History of Education* 22.3 (1993): 265–75.

Phillips, Mrs. Ellis L., Dean Mina Kerr, and Dean Agnes Wells. "History of the National Association of Deans of Women: Compiled February, 1926." *Proceedings of the Fourteenth Regular Meeting*, 228–35. Washington, D.C.: National Association of Deans of Women, 1927.

Pierce, Anna Eloise. *Deans and Advisers of Women and Girls*. New York: Professional and Technical Press, 1928.

Plastas, Melinda. *A Band of Noble Women: Racial Politics in the Women's Peace Movement*. Syracuse, N.Y.: Syracuse University Press, 2011.

Pochmara, Anna. *The Making of the New Negro: Black Authorship, Masculinity, and Sexuality in the Harlem Renaissance*. Amsterdam: Amsterdam University Press, 2012.

Porter, Charlotte W. "Physical Hindrances to Teaching Girls." *Forum* 12 (September 1891): 41–49.

Rasheed, Lisa R. "Lucy Diggs Slowe, Howard University Dean of Women, 1922–1937: Educator, Administrator, Activist." Ph.D. diss., Georgia State University, 2009. https://scholarworks.gsu.edu/eps_diss/55/.

Rasheed, Lisa R. "Lucy Diggs Slowe: Not a Matron but an Administrator." *African American Fraternities and Sororities*. Edited by Tamara L. Brown, Gregory S. Parks, and Clarenda M. Phillips, 249–66. Lexington: University Press of Kentucky, 2012.

Reid-Brinkley, Shanara R. "The Essence of Res(ex)pectability: Black Women's Negotiation of Black Femininity in Rap Music and Music Video." *Meridians* 8.1 (2008): 236–60.

Renetzky, Alvin, and Phyllis Ann Kaplan. *Standard Education Almanac*. Chicago: Marquis Academic Media, 1972.

Robertson, Nancy Marie. *Christian Sisterhood, Race Relations, and the YWCA, 1906–46*. Urbana: University of Illinois, 2007.

Robinson, Henry S. "The M Street High School, 1891–1916." *Records of the Columbia Historical Society, Washington, D.C.* 51 (1984): 119–43.

Robinson, Tracy, and Janie Victoria Ward. "'A Belief in Self Far Greater Than Anyone's Disbelief': Cultivating Resistance among African American Female Adolescents." In *Women, Girls and Psychotherapy: Reframing Resistance*. Edited by Carol Gilligan, Annie G. Rogers, and Deborah L. Tolman, 87–103. Binghamton, N.Y.: Harrington Park Press, 1991.

Rosenberry, Lois Kimball Mathews. *The Dean of Women*. Boston: Houghton Mifflin, 1915.

Ross, Marlon B. *Manning the Race: Reforming Black Men in the Jim Crow Era*. New York: New York University Press, 2004.

Sartorius, Kelly C. *Deans of Women and the Feminist Movement: Emily Taylor's Activism*. New York: Palgrave Macmillan, 2014.

Schmitt, Kaitlin. "Deans of Women in U.S. Higher Education." Ph.D. diss. Southern Illinois University, Carbondale, 2016.

Schumacher, Carolyn Sutcher. "The Open Gate." *Western Pennsylvania Historical Magazine* 69 (October 1986): 295–326.

Schwartz, Robert. *Deans of Men and the Shaping of Modern Culture*. New York: Palgrave Macmillan, 2010.

Schwartz, Robert. "Reconceptualizing the Leadership Roles of Women in Higher Education: A Brief History on the Importance of Deans of Women." *Journal of Higher Education* 68 (September-October 1997): 502–22.

"The Second Annual Howard Women's Dinner." *Howard University Record* 18.2 (1923): 148.

Shaw, Stephanie J. *What a Woman Ought to Be and Do: Black Professional Women Workers During the Jim Crow Era*. Chicago: University of Chicago Press, 1996.

"She Has Not Died In Vain." *Howard University Alumni Journal: The Case Against President Mordecai W. Johnson* (Winter 1937): 4.

Simmons, LaKisha Michelle. *Crescent City Girls: The Lives of Young Women in Segregated New Orleans*. Chapel Hill: University of North Carolina, 2015.

Simmons, LaKisha Michelle. "'To Lay Aside All Morals': Respectability, Sexuality and Black College Students in the United States in the 1930s." *Gender & History* 24.2 (2012): 431–55.

Slowe, Lucy Diggs. "Address Delivered by Soror Lucy D. Slowe at the Annual A.K.A. Boule Banquet." *Alpha Kappa Alpha Ivy Leaf*, December 1933, 19–20.

Slowe, Lucy Diggs. "The Colored Girl Enters College: What Shall She Expect?" *Opportunity: Journal of Negro Life* (September 1937): 276–79.

Slowe, Lucy Diggs. "The Dean of Women and Her Relation to the Personnel Office." In *Proceedings of the Fifteenth Annual Meeting of the National Association of Deans of Women, February 18–21, 1931*, 111–12. Washington, D.C.: National Association of Deans of Women, 1931.

Slowe, Lucy Diggs. "The Dean of Women in a Modern University." *Howard University Alumni Journal*, December 1933, 9–10.

Slowe, Lucy Diggs. "The Future of the Association of College Women." In *Proceedings of the Conference of College Women, Called by the College Alumnae Club, Washington, D.C., April 6 and 7, 1923*, 26–28. Washington, D.C.: Association of College Women, 1923.

Slowe, Lucy Diggs. "Higher Education of Negro Women." *Journal of Negro Education* 2.3 (1933): 352–58.

Slowe, Lucy Diggs. "The Place of the Dean of Women on the College Campus: Speech at Public Meeting of the Deans and Advisors in Colored Schools, Wilberforce University." *Journal of the College Alumnae Club of Washington*, memorial ed. (1939): 47–54.

Smith, Christi M. *Reparation and Reconciliation: The Rise and Fall of Integrated Higher Education*. Chapel Hill: University of North Carolina, 2016.

Smith, Jessie Carney, and Carrell Peterson Horton. *Historical Statistics of Black America*. New York: Gale Research, 1995.

Smith-Rosenberg, Carroll. *Disorderly Conduct: Visions of Gender in Victorian America*. New York: Oxford University Press, 1985.

Sturtevant, Sarah M. "The Qualifications and Preparation of Deans of Women." *Eleventh Yearbook of the National Association of Deans of Women*, 117–23. Washington, D.C.: NADW, 1924.

Talbot, Marion. *The Education of Women*. Chicago: University of Chicago Press, 1910.

Taylor, Traki L. "'Womanhood Glorified': Nannie Helen Burroughs and the National Training School for Women and Girls, Inc., 1909–1961." *Journal of African American History* 87 (2002): 390–402.

Tice, Karen W. *Queens of Academe: Beauty Pageantry, Student Bodies, and College Life*. New York: Oxford University Press, 2012.

"Tribute to Dean Slowe." *Journal of the College Alumnae Club of Washington*, memorial ed. (January 1939): 72–73.

"A Tribute to Soror Lucy D. Slowe." *Alpha Kappa Alpha Ivy Leaf* 15.4 (December 1937): 15, 34.

Turk, Diana B. *Bound by a Mighty Vow: Sisterhood and Women's Fraternities, 1870–1920*. New York: New York University Press, 2004.

"Undergraduate Life." *Howard University Record* 18.1 (1923): 86.

"University Notes." *Howard Alumnus*, May 15, 1925, 137.

"University Notes." *Howard University Record* 17.8 (June 1923): 430.

"Vocational Guidance: Our National Program." *Alpha Kappa Alpha Ivy Leaf* 5.1 (1926): 76–77.

Voigt, Irma E. "National Association of Deans of Women." *Occupations: The Vocational Guidance Journal* 15.8 (1937): 752–54.

Waite, Cally L. "DuBois and the Invisible Talented Tenth." In *Feminist Engagements: Reading, Registering, Reinvisioning Male Theorists in Education and Cultural Studies*. Edited by Kathleen Weiler, 33–45. New York: Routledge, 2001.

Warren, Stanley. "Black Behind the Black and Gold." DePauw University Archives, Greencastle, Ind., 1990. http://palni.contentdm.oclc.org/cdm/ref/collection/archives/id/120309.

Washington, Booker T. "Democracy and Education." Address Before the Institute of Arts and Sciences, Brooklyn, N.Y. September 30, 1896. https://teachingamericanhistory.org/library/document/democracy-and-education/.

Whitney, Mary E. "Women Student Personnel Administrators: The Past and Future." *Journal of College Student Personnel* 12 (January 1971): 8.

Williams, Fannie Barrier. "The Colored Girl." 1905. In Deegan, *Collected Writings of Fannie Barrier Williams*. Edited by Mary Jo Deegan, 63–66. DeKalb: Northern Illinois University Press, 2002.

Williams, Fannie Barrier. "The Intellectual Progress of the Colored Women of the United States Since the Emancipation Proclamation." 1894. In Deegan, *Collected Writings of Fannie Barrier Williams*, 17–27.

Wright, Marion Thompson. "Slowe, Lucy Diggs." In *Notable American Women: A Biographical Dictionary*, vol. 3, P–Z. Edited by Edward T. James, Janet Wilson James, and Paul S. Boyer, 299–300. Cambridge, Mass.: Harvard University Press, 1971.

Wright, Nazera Sadiq. *Black Girlhood in the Nineteenth Century*. Urbana: University of Illinois Press, 2016.

Yeboah, Amy Oppong. "Blueprint for Black Girl Magic: The Leadership of First Woman Dean of Howard University, Lucy Diggs Slowe." *Journal of the National Association of University Women* (Spring 2017–18): 9–17.

Zimmerman, Joan G. "Daughters of Main Street: Culture and the Female Community at Grinnel [*sic*], 1884–1917." In *Woman's Being, Woman's Place: Female Identity and Vocation in American History*. Edited by Mary Kelley, 154–70. Boston: G. K. Hall, 1977.

INDEX

147

snubbed by, 102; clash over Mills, 91–92; deathbed ultimatum, 101; housing order against L. D. Slowe, 97–100; patriarchal attitudes of, 11, 55, 92; pay raise denial, 100–101; persecution and, 92–101; removal of deans from university council, 92–93; Women's Department gutted by, 93–97

Julian, Mattie, ix–x
Julian, Percy, 38
Justiss, Valarie O'Mega, 88

Kappa Alpha Theta, ix
Kerr, Mina, 88–89

Lindsey, Treva, 8, 24
Living more abundantly philosophy, 3–4, 45–50, 110–112; deaning and, 10; departure from respectability, 53–59, 89; New Howard Woman and, 6–7, 51, 59, 84; New Negro Woman and, 11–12
Locke, Alain, 38; *The New Negro*, 85. *See also* New Negro
Locke, Bettie, ix

McDougald, Elise Johnson: on Black men, 29; on struggle of Black women, 85–86; "The Task of Negro Womanhood," 29
McNeill, Bertha, 2, 113n2, 133n13
Miller, Carroll L. L., 7
Miller, Kelly, 38, 93; on L. D. Slowe as dean, 105–106
Mills, Clarence H.: Burrill attacked by, 91; M. W. Johnson and, 91–92; L. D. Slowe attacked by, 90–92; student complaints against, 90, 129–130n34
Morgan State College, 80, 101; L. D. Slowe's papers initially deposited at, 129n18
M Street Junior High / Robert Gould Shaw School: curriculum of, 34; junior high school philosophy, 33–34; L. D. Slowe as principal, 33–35
Murphy, Ella, 106
Murphy, Valeria, ix–x
Murphy, Vashti Turley, 109

NACW. *See* National Association of College Women

NADW. *See* National Association of Deans of Women
National Association of College Women (NACW), 10, 51–52; charge to, 62; promotion of deaning at HBCUs, 53, 86
National Association of Deans of Women (NADW), 10; Blanchard on, 77–79; founding of, 18–19, 127–128n76; segregation and racism in, 74–82; Women's Campus visit, 60–61
National Association of Women's Deans and Advisors of Colored Schools (NAWDACS), 10, 52, 53; address to, 83; names for, 122–123n79
National Council on Colored Work, 68
National Student Council (NSC), 68, 72, 77
National Training School for Women and Girls, 30–31
NAWDACS. *See* National Association of Women's Deans and Advisors of Colored Schools
Neale, Mamie Geraldine, 36–37, 40
New Howard Woman: distinction from sororal womanhood, 50–51; expectations for, 58–59, 111–112; as New Negro Woman, 8, 35, 112; promotion through Women's Dinner, 4–7, 36–45; L. D. Slowe ideal of, 36–37; students embrace of, 36–37, 108; vocational counseling for, 56–58
New Negro, 11; Locke, A., on, 85; patriarchal attitudes of, 84–86, 106
New Negro, The (Locke, A.), 85
New Negro Woman: assertions of voice and equality, 24–27; Black girlhood focus, 27–29; distinction from respectability, 5; New Howard Woman as, 8, 35, 112; patriarchal resistance to, 11; philosophy of, 5–6, 8–9; L. D. Slowe as, 31–35, 51, 77; vision of higher education, 53–58; in Washington, D.C., 29–31
New Woman, 8; color line and, 17, 62–66, 70; deaning and, 9, 18–23; education for growth and social usefulness, 16–17; emergence of, 15. *See also* National Association of Deans of Women
NSC (National Student Council), 68, 72, 77

Oberlin College, 17, 25

CPSIA information can be obtained
at www.ICGtesting.com
Printed in the USA
LVHW102105200323
742053LV00004B/705

9 780820 361659